THE STOIC TEACHER

ANCIENT MIND HACKS TO HELP EDUCATORS FOSTER RESILIENCY, OPTIMISM, AND INNER CALM

PROFESSIONAL DEVELOPMENT TITLES BY ALPHABET PUBLISHING

The Teacher Self-Care Manual by Patrice Palmer

Keeping the Essence in Sight by Sharon Hartle

Classroom Community Builders by Walton Burns

We are a small, independent publishing company that specializes in creative resources for teachers in the area of English Language Arts and English as a Second or Other Language. We help stock the teacher toolkit with practical, useful, and innovative materials.

Sign up for our mailing list on our website for teaching tips, updates on new books, and for discounts and giveaways you won't find anywhere else.

ADVANCE PRAISE

Ryan Racine's short book deftly distills Stoic theory and practice for busy teachers so they can start applying it to their lives ASAP.
— Gregory Lopez, Author *A Handbook for New Stoics*

The Stoic Teacher *goes beyond the usual books on pedagogy and instead shows us how to maintain our own sense of equanimity and true inner peace in an increasingly challenging classroom.*
— Donna Quesada, author *Buddha in the Classroom*

The Stoic Teacher *by Ryan Racine will not only inspire you to come to school with the strength to overcome obstacles, but it will also equip you with 'Mental hacks' that will get you through even the worst days.*
— Robert Dunlop, Author *Strive for Happiness in Education*

Teaching is a tough job. The Stoic Teacher will give you the tools to overcome difficulties and thrive in the classroom.
— *Steve Karafit,* The Sunday Stoic

I cannot wait to use the tools and recommendations, and to put into practice everything from the journaling framework ... to the wise reflection on what could happen in the future!
— Ruth Pearce, CIO of ALLE, LLC, Coach, Speaker, Author

[this book] reveals how adopting Stoicism as his "life philosophy" changed his perspective on teaching. As a Stoic, one is not "looking for a job that brings you happiness all the time instead one that allows you to be your best self."
— Ranjini George, MA, MFA, PhD, University of Toronto

This book is excellent. I enjoyed it immensely. Beginning teachers and seasoned veterans alike should read it,
— Robert J. Marzano, Chief Academic Officer, Marzano Resources, author *The New Art and Science of Teaching*

Ryan Racine's The Stoic Teacher *is a quick, value-packed read and is organized in a way that teachers will appreciate. Each chapter is on-point and relevant, and each contains actionable homework that will help transform Stoic concepts into daily practice.*
— Jeff MacLoud, teacher, school director, and entrepenur

THE STOIC TEACHER

ANCIENT MIND
HACKS TO HELP
EDUCATORS
FOSTER RESILIENCY,
OPTIMISM, AND
INNER CALM

RYAN RACINE

ISBN: 978-1-956159-12-7 (print)
       978-1-956159-16-5 (ebook)

Alphabet Publishing
29 Milo Drive
Branford, CT 06405
USA

info@alphabetpublishingbooks.com
www.AlphabetPublish.com

Discounts on class sets and bulk orders available upon inquiry.

Book Cover Design by Melissa Williams Design
Interior Design by Red Panda Editorial Services

Country of Manufacture Specified on Last Page
First Printing 2022

CONTENTS

PREFACE

During teachers college, I studied a lot of education theory. I read the works of thinkers like John Dewey, Henry Giroux, and bell hooks and was constantly asked to question the many traditional teaching methods and assessment practices that educators still use within schools. I was told to be an innovative teacher, one who would foster equitable opportunities for student learning. While these theoretical and pedagogical ideas excited me, something was noticeably missing from each of my course syllabi: a focus on the mental side of the profession. For instance, at no time did we discuss how to remain calm when a student swears at you or ways to stay optimistic after one of your lessons does not go according to plan.

Throughout my career, I have experienced those stresses and more at some point or another. During my first year of teaching, I realized that the idealized classroom I had dreamt of for a long time was far from realistic, especially when teaching a class where some of my students regularly misbehaved toward any sort of authority figure. I often walked into class wanting to be the next Mr. Keaton from Dead Poets Society and left feeling disappointed and belittled, questioning whether I was actually making a difference in my students' lives and—on a more personal level—whether I was meant to be a teacher.

I have had numerous conversations with teachers who are five to ten years away from retirement and feel burnt out. I could tell that they had become dissatisfied with their job and were just riding it out until they had enough money saved up to call it quits. While I am grateful that I have never felt this way so far in my career, I can empathize with them. I too have faced difficult situations in the classroom when I wished the clock would tick away just a little bit faster. When I first experienced these stressful moments, I blamed the school, the system, and the kids. I complained to my colleagues that we did not have enough resources, lacked proper support in the classroom, and uttered generalizations about how most of today's students cannot focus on a task for more than five minutes. What I never considered, however, was that something else could be influencing my pessimist mindset. It was not until I started reading Stoic philosophy (particularly the works of Marcus Aurelius, Epictetus, and Seneca) that I began to re-examine whether I was contributing to my own frustration.

I never formally studied Stoic philosophy in school. In fact, the only mention of Stoicism came when one of my English professors briefly alluded to it during a lecture on William Shakespeare. It was not until a ranting session with a close friend about the proposed cuts that our government was making to the education sector, ones that would directly impact my chances of obtaining full-time employment over the next number of years, that I first was introduced to one of the main lessons of Stoicism.

"Yes, these cuts seem bad," he said, "but it is out of your control. Why bother worrying about something that you cannot change?"

I initially responded to his advice with displeasure. After all, how could I just roll over and pretend like things were fine and dandy when my future was at stake? Did I spend six years and thousands of dollars on my education to work precarious jobs here and there in order to scrape together a decent, liveable wage?

"No, you don't have to tell yourself that everything is perfect. Instead, you must understand that at this moment, you cannot do anything about these cuts. Therefore, focus your attention on something that you can change, like bettering yourself as a teacher and a person," my friend said.

I mulled over his words that night and though my perspective on things did not change the following day, the initial Stoic seed was planted, one that would eventually grow into not only a fascination of the philosophy but a willingness to live out its core principles and teachings.

What is Stoic Philosophy?

The English word, "philosophy", is a combination of two Greek words: *philo* (meaning love), and *sophia* (meaning wisdom). Therefore, philosophy can be defined as the love of wisdom. Such a definition, however, still tells us very little about philosophy's purpose. If you were to take a modern philosophy class in university, you would probably be learning about a number of scientific, political, and metaphysical topics that can help you to understand the world in more complex ways. It would, however, do little in providing you suggestions for how to live well. In contrast, ancient schools of philosophical thought, particularly Stoicism, focus on this very idea.

Stoicism was founded around 301 BCE in Athens, Greece by a man named Zeno of Citium. Zeno was a merchant travelling from Phoenicia to the Greek port of Piraeus when he ended up getting shipwrecked, losing his wealth in the process. This apparent misfortune, however, did not plunge Zeno into a deep depression but instead propelled him to live more reflectively. He ended up spending the next twenty years in Athens, studying under the most influential thinkers there, including the philosopher Crates. Zeno would go on to give lectures in the Athenian city centre under a public colonnade known as the *Stoa Poikile*, or painted porch. Hence, the name "Stoic", derived from *stoa*, was born.

Zeno, along with the other first Stoic philosophers, was inspired by the Greek thinker Socrates and his mission to live a good life. How might we go about living a good life according to the Stoics?

Thinking through problems in a rational manner and following a set of defined virtues is a good start. This does not involve repressing our emotions, unlike a popular misconception of what it means to be Stoic. The Stoics are also famous for embracing hardship. We see this principle resonating in Marcus Aurelius's Meditations. Marcus was the emperor of Rome from 161 to 180 CE. His Meditations is a composition of his own personal reflections that he wrote during his stressful administration. The interesting thing is that he did not intend them to be released to the public, so in a sense we are reading the journal entries of one of the most notable figures in history. "The impediment to action advances action," he famously wrote, "What stands in the way becomes the way" (5.20). Marcus here is reminding himself how obstacles can be viewed as opportunities for us to reinvent ourselves and grow, a central tenant in Stoic philosophy.

Besides the former Roman emperor, the two other ancient Stoic philosophers that I will be referring to throughout this book are Seneca and Epictetus. Seneca was not only a philosopher but also a renowned playwright. Many of his writings were focused on heavy topics like dealing with grief, anger, and death. Seneca also worked as an advisor to the infamous Emperor Nero. You can imagine, therefore, how stressful his job would have been, considering Nero was known as a cruel ruler who not only had his own mother killed but eventually ordered Seneca to death as well (at the time, Nero wrongfully believed that Seneca was conspiring against him).

Epictetus, the third major Stoic philosopher, was born a slave (his name actually means "acquired"). After Nero died, however, Epictetus was freed from slavery and started his own school of Stoic philosophy where he taught for around twenty-five years until he was eventually banned from Rome and forced to move to Nicopolis, Greece. Like Socrates, Epictetus did not write anything down. All of his writings, including the *Discourses* and *Enchiridion*, were recorded by his student Arrian.

While Stoicism lost its popularity when Marcus died in 180 BCE (the rise of Christianity also helped put a halt to the widespread practice of the philosophy), it has made a major resurgence over the past fifty years or so, influencing many thinkers in self-help circles and helping to shape Cognitive Behavioural Therapy. Readerly interest in the philosophy has also grown significantly over the past decade. I am sure that if you visit your local bookshop, you will come across a number of titles with the word "Stoic" in it. *The Daily Stoic, A Guide to the Good Life: The Ancient Art of Stoic Joy*, and *How to be a Stoic: Using Ancient Philosophy to Live a Modern Life* are just a few noteworthy ones.

The Purpose and Layout of this Book

This book does not provide pedagogical methods about how to be a more engaging teacher or strategies to help manage behaviours in the classroom. There are many more qualified and experienced individuals out there who have written about these topics in great detail. Instead, each chapter will focus on cognitive tools (or "mental hacks") to help teachers remain resilient, even in the worst of situations. These tools have something in common: they all originate from Stoic philosophy.

I will start the book by looking at Stoicism's relevance to our jobs while also discussing the four Stoic virtues in the introduction. Chapter one will then focus on how we can go about preparing for the school day in a Stoic manner. I will talk about the importance of journaling every morning, premeditating on adversity, and focusing on the things within our control. Chapter two will look at how to keep our cool in the midst of stressful situations at work. Chapter three will introduce Stoic strategies, such as reflecting on our value judgements, to help teachers reframe a "bad day." Chapter three will look at the importance of finding a role model or creating your own Stoic sage (I will get into what the latter term means later on). Chapter five will focus on how to deal with imposter syndrome. Chapter six will look at the importance of self-care and chapter seven will include a variety of Stoic resources for your own professional development. The last chapter of the book will contain some firsthand narratives from a number of teachers who use Stoic philosophy to help them navigate the demands of their job. Most chapters contain writing exercises to help reinforce and make the Stoic principles applicable. As well, I have included end-of-chapter reflection questions that you can ask yourself or use as jumping-off points for discussion if you are reading this book in a group setting.

Just a last note before you start the introduction: while you are reading the book, feel free to discard the bits of advice you disagree with or find irrelevant to your current situation. The great thing about the Stoic philosophers is that they did not consider their words to be doctrinal and were open to being challenged. Nonetheless, Stoic philosophy has shaped my worldview for the better and, in my opinion, it can help influence others. Whether you teach in a public-school setting, academia, or some other unconventional way, I hope there is something you can take from the following chapters that will help you keep on keeping on!

STOICISM'S RELEVANCE TO TEACHING

O ne of my favourite things to do outside of teaching is run. The initial reason I got into running was to lose the weight that I put on in university. I started my running journey a couple of years ago by making it a routine to go to my local gym each morning with a friend who had the same goal of losing weight. Once we got to the gym, we would spend anywhere from ten to thirty minutes jogging on a treadmill. After a little while, though, this routine got a bit boring, and I switched to running outside. I am glad that I made this change because doing so helped spark my immense love for running. Running became not just a means to losing weight but something that I enjoyed doing for its own sake. I started exploring different paths in my city and signed up for a number of outdoor races, including a 10K, half-marathon, and eventually a full marathon.

I have only been running consistently for a small portion of my life, yet people always ask me to give them tips as if I am some sort of high-performance athlete (trust me, I am far from it). The two most common questions I am asked are:

1. What advice would I give a beginner trying to set up a training plan?
2. How does one stay motivated to continue running, especially in the winter months?

I find the second question a lot more philosophical to answer than the first. The reason is because in order to remain a consistent runner, I argue, that one has to imbue meaning in the very act of putting one foot in front of the other. While some may find losing weight a sufficient reason to continue running, there is a decent chance that this motive will not be sustainable. After all, if you lose the weight, then what? For me, I now view running as a way to practice discipline and patience. For example, convincing oneself to run that extra mile when it is pouring rain outside can help to cultivate inner strength that can also be used when faced with other obstacles in life.

Why Teach?

I started the chapter by talking about running because just as I argue it is important to develop a *why* for something like running, I believe the same must be said about teaching. In fact, my motivation for running and teaching are similar. Just as I do not run solely for health reasons, I certainly do not teach for perks like the summers off. Instead, one of the many reasons that I teach is because this profession provides me with a deep sense of fulfilment. In particular, being a teacher allows me the opportunity to make a difference in young people's lives. At the same time, I have learned in my short time teaching that my job is not always sunshine and rainbows. As I am writing this, my class is made up of students who have either been suspended or expelled from their designated high school. You can imagine, therefore, some of the behavioural issues that I have to deal with on a daily basis. I have noticed that there is a high staff turnover rate in this specialized program, mainly because teachers get burnt out. I do not blame them! It is mentally exhausting to plan for and manage many of the students who are enrolled in our classrooms. When I get bogged down during a tough day at work, the thing that keeps me going is reminding myself of my why.

A Stoic Approach to Teaching

How is Stoicism relevant to teachers? One way is that it can help to inform your why for teaching. Going back to my first year of teaching, there were times when I thought that I was working in the wrong field because I spent most of my day managing student behaviours rather than actually teaching the curriculum. Since we live in a world obsessed with instant gratification, I expected that unless I was feeling positive emotions every second of the day, I was missing out on something and wasting my life. My perspective on things changed when I took on Stoicism as my life philosophy. Taking on this Stoic approach means that you are not necessarily looking for a job that brings you happiness all of the time but instead one that allows you to be your best self. Just because you face significant challenges at work (such as dealing with uncooperative students or staff) does not mean you are in the wrong field! If you believe that teaching is your passion, you must expect hardships will come with the job. After all, the word "passion" come from the Latin, *pati*—which means "to suffer".

Eudaimonia and the Four Stoic Virtues

The Stoics argued that life's goal is to strive towards *eudaimonia*, which involves cultivating the best qualities within us. The Greek translation itself comes out to mean being good (*eu*) with your inner spirit (*daimon*).

To help us reach *eudaimonia*, the Stoics laid out four distinct virtues that we should follow in order to reach our best selves:

1. **Wisdom** is thought to be the most important Stoic virtue. It can allow us to make logical decisions, sound judgements, and help challenge past beliefs. Wisdom can also be practiced by the constant pursuit of knowledge so that we can expand our mind to different perspectives. Hopefully the Stoic practices that you will be learning about within this book can help to cultivate a sense of wisdom both inside and outside of the classroom. Of course, reading and learning about other non-Stoic topics can also help us to grow wise!

2. **Justice** means doing the right thing from an ethical perspective. It is about knowing how to act in order to contribute the best we can to the world. If we are bringing integrity to our job, the teaching profession itself can provide us with opportunities to practice justice. We can also practice justice by doing things like listening to and elevating the voices of the marginalized, especially those of our own students.

3. **Courage** helps us act against injustices and persist even in the midst of obstacles and setbacks. It does not include, however, the elimination of fear or anxiety. Agreeing to take on a difficult class when it is offered to you by your school principal is a great example of being courageous. Though you know it may cause future strife, the decision to say "yes" is a noble act and will make you a better teacher and person in the long run. The same thing can be said when undertaking tasks that push you past your comfort zone, like coaching a sport you have never actually played.

4. **Temperance,** or moderation, includes exercising self-discipline, control, and awareness to help control our impulses so that we focus on the long term over the short term. By practicing temperance, we turn away from excesses and focus on the essentials. Perhaps you switch school districts because doing so will allow for a quicker commute. You may have been closer to getting on permanently in the other district, but you know down the road this switch will significantly benefit your family situation. In addition, exercising temperance can involve responding to challenges from the classroom or from administration and not flying off the handle and getting angry right away. Temperance also involves tempering expectations for our students and ourselves and learning how to strike a balance in life.

Use the chart below to brainstorm the values that are most important to you (i.e. being a good co-worker, being compassionate

VALUES THAT ARE IMPORTANT TO ME	HOW THESE VALUES REINFORCE MY *WHY* FOR TEACHING

towards your students, etc.) If you want, you can reference and build off of the Stoic virtues discussed above. Clarifying your values can help to formulate strong why statements.

Conclusion

The Stoics believed that following a set of strong virtues has a great impact on living our best selves. We should start reflecting on what it means to be virtuous because doing so can help us to find our why for getting up in the morning and, in turn, flourish within our profession. Having a strong why can also make the practices that I will be getting into easier to implement.

End-of-Chapter Reflection Questions

* Why is teaching meaningful to you? If it is not meaningful to you right now, reflect on the reasons why you got into the profession.
* What does it mean to live your best self as a teacher?
* Are you burnt out or has teaching ever left you feeling burnt out? What led you to feeling this way?
* What do you want out of your teaching career?
* What Stoic virtue(s) do you find yourself cultivating today?
* What ones(s) do you wish to cultivate in the future?

CHAPTER ONE

PREPARING FOR THE SCHOOL DAY

"When you first rise in the morning tell yourself: I will encounter busybodies, ingrates, egomaniacs, liars, the jealous, and cranks. They are all stricken with these afflictions because they don't know the difference between good and evil."

— Marcus Aurelius

Teachers have a busy and stressful job. Between planning, marking, supervision duties, and extra-curriculars, our schedule can be action-packed. Therefore, it can be very difficult to find the opportunity to reflect and mentally prepare for the day. Knowing this, the Stoics believed that one of the best times to look inward, examine, and reflect is first thing in the morning. Implementing and following a well thought-out morning routine can enable us to get a head start on the day, as opposed to waking up with little time to spare before the craziness begins. It also allows us to attain a small victory before we leave our home, and this feeling can lead to a positive domino effect.

Before you continue reading the rest of this chapter, take a few moments to think about what your current morning routine looks like and whether it needs to be changed. Do you find yourself rushing to get to school? Do you feel that this rushing ultimately influences your mindset in some sort of negative way (i.e., maybe you are less patient with students, less open-minded, etc.)? Right now, I try to follow the same morning routine every day. It consists of waking up at 6 am, reading nonfiction, occasionally exercising, meditating, and lastly showering. I have not always had this routine, and I am sure it will change at some point, but since I implemented it, I find that my workday goes a lot more smoothly.

The Power of Journaling

Many contemporary Stoic thinkers such as Ryan Holiday recommend journaling shortly after waking up to help get ourselves focused on the day's tasks. We can journal in a number of ways, such as typing in a computer document, talking into a voice recorder, or writing in a good old-fashioned book (I have done all three at some point or another, but now I use a book and a nice fountain pen to help make the process more enjoyable). When I journal, I address the following topics:

1. I list at least one thing that went well yesterday. This could be a lesson that resonated with my students, a heartfelt or honest conversation that I had with a fellow colleague, or a memorable moment that took place during an extra-curricular activity after school.

2. I list at least one thing that I wish I handled better from yesterday. This could be undeservedly yelling at a student, not being as prepared as I should have been to deliver a lesson, or talking badly about a fellow staff member to someone else.

3. I write down strategies that I could use to improve myself as

a teacher and prevent these above issues from reoccurring. I tend to resort to the Stoic strategies from this book or CBT-based ones, but feel free to use other ones as well.

4. I write at least one thing that I am grateful for. For me, this is the easiest prompt to answer, but one that I tend to neglect the most, especially when I am stressed. If, for some reason, I cannot think of anything, I give thanks for having the opportunity to work since some I know do not have a job or one that they find even remotely fulfilling.

Expect the Worst

According to the Stoics, the most important strategy to use while preparing for the day is what Seneca calls *premeditatio malorum*, which means to premeditate on future adversities. This practice involves imagining what you believe to be the worst-case scenario that could arise from a particular event and being willing to accept the outcome. For example, if you are rehearsing a lesson, consider the possibility that your students will not be receptive to your ideas and questions.

This kind of thinking may seem pessimistic, but it is far from it. In his *Letters*, Seneca outlines the benefits of premeditating on adversity. "The wise person gets used to future evils: what other people make bearable by long endurance, he makes bearable by long reflection," Seneca writes. He goes on to say that "we sometimes hear the inexperienced say, 'I didn't know this was in store for me.' The wise person knows that everything is in store for him. Whatever happens, he says, 'I knew'" (76.34).

Premeditating on adversity is not about continually obsessing over what could seemingly go wrong but instead having, using the words of William Irvine, "a flickering thought" about it. Unlike pessimistic thinking, you are not under the impression that bad things will inevitably happen but have an understanding that it is a possibility. The main psychological benefit of this mental exercise is to help soften the blow if something occurs that is not considered "good" in our eyes because we already expected it.

Below, you can find the two-step process I follow to practice premeditating on adversity in my journal:

1. I first predict what potential difficult events could arise throughout the school day. I ensure that these predictions are made based on previous evidence. For example, if a student misbehaved yesterday, I assume they might do it again today. If a fellow colleague ignored me in the hallway, I will expect the same behaviour in the future. I usually make a list of these events without going overboard (maybe two to three things per day).

2. I then write about how I could respond in the moment if these events were to occur. I rehearse these responses so that if they do take place, I have a script to fall back on. My reactions usually involve me staying calm and not resorting to outward anger. For example, if a colleague snubs me, I might write that I will nod my head and continue walking. I can always take time to process it later but in the moment, lashing out will not get me anywhere.

Let's Practice!

Take time now to practice journaling! I have created a sample template on the next page with some of the prompts. You can write directly in the book or use it as a guide for your own approach to journaling. I also include a section on premeditating on adversity.

DATE	WHAT IS ONE THING YOU ARE GRATEFUL FOR?

LIST AT LEAST ONE THING THAT WENT WELL YESTERDAY IN THE CLASSROOM:

LIST AT LEAST ONE THING THAT YOU COULD HAVE HANDLED BETTER:

WHAT STRATEGIES CAN YOU USE TO IMPROVE AS A TEACHER AND AVOID THESE ABOVE ISSUES?

PREMEDITATING ON ADVERSITY

POTENTIAL ADVERSITIES	HOW I WILL RESPOND

Focus on the Things Within Your Control

Epictetus said that undesirable emotions are often caused by a failure to obtain something external. He argued that we should not want things to be in our power which are not in our power but instead concern ourselves with matters that we have direct influence over. This idea, known as the dichotomy of control, is central to Stoicism

The dichotomy of control is all about making the best use of what is in our power and taking the rest as it happens. In particular, we should focus on doing the work in whatever endeavour we are pursuing instead of being preoccupied with the fruits of our labour. According to the Stoics, we must take any intended or unintended outcomes with equanimity because they are beyond our control. This principle is easier said than done, but it can help simplify our life. Here are some examples of things that are within and outside of your control, according to the Stoics.

Complete Control	Incomplete Control
* how we think about a situation * how we respond to a situation * our intentions	* our health * our possessions * how others perceive us * our working conditions

The dichotomy of control truly helped me to take a step forward towards alleviating the stress that comes with being a teacher, especially stress related to budget cuts, class sizes, and criticism from parents, co-workers, and students. I recommend reading *A Handbook for New Stoics: How to Thrive in a World Out of Your Control—52 Week-by-Week Lessons* by Massimo Pigliucci and

Gregory Lopez to learn about some practical and easy to follow exercises that help to illustrate this principle. One of the exercises they recommend is to make a T-chart before leaving home for the day. You can then document different occurrences that are expected to take place and sort which ones are under your control and which ones are not. For example, if you have a staff meeting to attend at school for 8 am, intending to show up on time is under your control but actually showing up on time is not (since factors like heavy traffic can stop this from happening). By writing these events out and making this separation, you can internalize what is under your control and what is not, which in turn "give[s] you a clearer picture of what exactly you should focus your desires and aversions on to achieve peace of mind" (Pigliucci & Lopez, 19).

When I started applying to different teaching jobs, I employed a similar writing tactic in my journal. For example, I categorized preparing for each interview as something I should focus on while worrying about whether I would get the job or not as something I should avoid doing. I found that by considering the dichotomy of control, the preparation process became easier. I felt like a weight was lifted off my shoulders due to not worrying about the outcome of the interview. As a result, the interviews themselves became more enjoyable experiences because I remained more present throughout them and did not get hung up on whether I said the right or wrong things. By switching my mindset on the things that I could control, I soon became more grateful for the opportunity to even be able to apply to a posting rather than complaining about the lack of teaching jobs.

Each morning, take time to separate what may be in your control that day from what is not. You can again use your journal or even write this exercise out on the chalkboard (I have done the latter a number of times when no one is in the classroom except myself). Here is an example:

Event	What are the things within my control?	What are the things outside of my control?

As Stoic teachers, it is imperative to use our mental energy to focus on what is under our complete control. It is not that we stop caring about things that we can't control, but rather that we come to a deep understanding that our happiness is not dependent on them. Try to make giving it your best shot the goal and do not get attached to the external outcome. That way, you can maintain your tranquility while also giving yourself the best possible chance to succeed.

Goal Setting and the Stoic Reverse Clause

While we are preparing for the day, it is always a good idea to set goals. Of course, from a Stoic perspective, we should be trying our best to set goals that are within our control. Take a moment to reflect upon the type of goals that you set for yourself each day as a teacher. Are they within your control? If not, you risk setting yourself up for frustration when things do not go according to plan. I know that early in my career, I would always try to set a goal that my students would behave in class. When a student misbehaved, I automatically blamed myself and felt like a failure. If I simply phrased the goal as "I will reinforce expected behaviours with my class and implement my new management strategy with my students," I would have set myself up for a higher percentage of success because the goal was completely up to me.

Try completing the exercise below. It involves getting you to practice reframing goals so that they are under your control.

Inital Goal	Reframed Goal
I will become the new program chair of my department.	I will complete the program chair application document to the best of my abilities.
I will get my students to behave appropriately during our second period assembly.	
My class will score high on the standardized test next week.	

Obviously, not all of the goals that we set for ourselves will be within our control. We may have one or two lofty goals that we wish to attain one day, and that's okay. I know I would love to teach high school music full-time in the future. There are things within my control to get there, such as accepting part-time teaching sections of music whenever they are offered to me in order to gain more experience as well as practicing as often as I can on instruments that are less familiar to me so that I can become an all-around better musician, but ultimately this goal is contingent on many external factors. For these types of goals, the Stoics advise us to use a reverse clause, which is to add a disclaimer like "fate permitting" or "God willing" to your goal. While it may seem silly, doing so will help us realize that if things do not go according to plan, it is not entirely our fault. Try adding a reverse clause to the goals you craft for yourself that in some way rely on external factors.

Start the Day in Discomfort

Epictetus said that "we must endure a winter training and can't be dashing into situations for which we aren't yet prepared" (*Discourses,*10). In this short quote, Epictetus is referring to the Stoic practice of voluntary discomfort. Adding discomfort to your morning routine may sound rather counterintuitive but hear me out. This practice involves undertaking a particular activity that we are not fond of in order to cultivate resiliency. That can help to prepare us for even larger stresses throughout the day. This does not entail, however, doing something that will push us to our absolute limit. A cold shower (even for ten seconds), exercising in some way before work, or getting up a little bit earlier than we usually do bring about small but manageable stressors. Pushing through one or more of these self-made obstacles will provide a small victory in the morning and can have a significant ripple effect for the rest of the day. We can tell ourselves that "I perse-vered through _____; therefore, I can deal with this situation in the classroom."

To help decide upon a discomfort for the morning, fill out the below prompts:

List of discomforts you can manage undertaking each morning:

_____

_____

_____

Choose one of the discomforts above. What action plan would you put in place to implement it (i.e., when will you undergo the discomfort)?

_____

_____

_____

What will you tell yourself to help you persevere? You might want to think about why you are going to pursue this kind of voluntary discomfort.

_____

_____

_____

Conclusion

If there is anything I would like you to take away from this chapter, it is to not go about showing up to school on autopilot. The Stoics advise us to try to add a bit more awareness to your mornings, even if it is a matter of finding a quiet place to reflect and mentally rehearse the day and possible obstacles that you may face for a couple minutes before your students enter the door.

End-of-Chapter Reflection Questions

* How can having a strong morning routine help increase the probability that you can be your best self at school?
* What does your morning routine look like?
* Do you feel you should make changes to your morning routine? If so, what one practice from this chapter do you believe you can implement as early as this week?
* How can you keep yourself accountable?
* Do you find yourself struggling with worrying about things outside of your control? If yes, why do you think this happens?

CHAPTER TWO

STAYING CALM IN THE CLASSROOM

"It is the mark of a great mind to rise above insults."

— Seneca

I remember it like it was yesterday. During my first year of teaching, a student of mine got into trouble at recess and was forced to spend the rest of the day in the vice-principal's office. As a result, I had to prepare a package of work for her. While going through her desk to gather her notebooks, another student (one who always found a way to get on my nerves) kept pestering me about what I was doing and whether the student who was in trouble was getting suspended. After about thirty seconds, I ended up screaming at him with all of my might, saying something to the effect of "it is none of your business!" He left the room crying and I immediately felt a great sense of guilt.

Looking back at the situation, I know that I could have handled things a lot better. At the time, however, I did not have the tools or experience to better deal with the type of pressure that I was under. Teaching is one of the most difficult jobs out there because we cannot simply hide under our desk or take ten minutes off to reflect on how to respond when we find ourselves in challenging situations. Instead, we have to take preemptive steps to help prepare ourselves for remaining calm in the moment.

The Stoic Perspective on Anger

I have noticed that much of the stress that I experience during the school day is a result of me being angry at someone. Besides the above example with my student, I have displayed outward anger towards many other students in my career who have either not been on task, been defiant towards me, or have complained about the marks I gave them. I'm not proud of that but it does happen and I am sure many teachers can relate.

The Stoics believed that anger is one of the most dangerous emotions. In fact, Seneca wrote a whole essay dedicated to anger and thought of it as temporary madness. He, along with Epictetus and Marcus Aurelius, believed that anger makes us vulnerable because it can lead to irrational thinking and the forming of cognitive biases. I have been in many situations, especially early in my career, where a student says something to me (such as how much they hate school and following rules) and my mind automatically starts spinning out of control about how they are a troubled person and will probably not amount to anything in the future. Obviously, thoughts like these are problematic and inaccurate, but anger can have that effect on us. One way that I have worked towards developing a healthier mindset when I start feeling angry in the classroom is practicing what Donald Robertson calls "Stoic Mindfulness".

Stoic Mindfulness

In his essay "A Simplified Modern Approach to Stoicism," Donald Robertson outlines how to apply Stoic Mindfulness to our day. "When you experience a distressing or problematic thought," he writes, "pause, and tell yourself: 'This is just a thought and not at all the things it claims to represent'" (n.p.). Robertson is reminding us that it is not things that upset us but our judgements about things (I will get more into this idea in the next chapter). In a similar way, Epictetus says we must train ourselves to respond to negative thoughts with the mantra "you are merely an appearance and in no way the thing appearing" (*Enchiridion,* 1.1.). Simply put, the Stoics emphasize that thoughts are not facts. This strategy can help us to detach from our initial impressions and work towards remaining calm in the classroom.

Rather than being carried away by our initial impressions, we can postpone our response for at least a few seconds or so, waiting until our feelings have slightly settled down and we are able to view things more rationally and objectively before deciding what action to take. Seneca echoes this idea when he writes that the "best corrective of anger lies in delay" (*On Anger,* 2.29.1). Relatedly, Epictetus told his students that they should spot automatic thoughts and feelings when they arise and refrain from allowing themselves to be swept along with them. As Stoic teachers, we can tell ourselves that if a particular problem is really important, we will choose to think about it when we are ready, rather than allowing it to hijack our train of thought. That way we can give it our full attention and evaluate it more calmly and rationally, perhaps during our after-school reflection (see next chapter).

Focus on the Present Moment

Another strategy to keep us grounded during stressful situations is to focus on the present moment. "Keep this in mind," Aurelius wrote, "that each of us lives only this present and indivisible moment. Everything else has either already been lived or is uncertain" (*Meditations,* 3.10). The Stoics naturally focused their attention on the present because they believed that only our actions in the here and now are up to us. The most important thing in life, our ability to strive towards our best self, resides squarely in the present moment. If you worry about what happened five minutes ago in the staffroom or you wish that the day would go by more quickly, you are not setting yourself up to live your best self because your attention will be shifted elsewhere.

There are different tricks that we can use to focus on the present moment when we are teaching (check out Lisa J. Lucas's book *Practicing Presence: Simple Self-Care Strategies for Teachers* or Donna Quesada's *Buddha in the Classroom: Zen Wisdom to Inspire Teachers* to learn about some of these!). One thing that works for me is to bring attention to my own breathing. If I get into a stressful situation at work, like one of my students is running around the school instead of coming back to class, I focus on my breath while handling the issue because it is something that I have control over. Here is another exercise mentioned by Donald Robertson to help focus on the present moment as well as practicing the previously mentioned strategy of detaching from our initial judgements:

1. Stop what you're doing for a moment or more if you want.
2. Turn your attention inward and focus on observing your own mental activity, from moment to moment, keeping your attention firmly grounded in the here and now.
3. Don't try to change anything or stop anything from changing. Just notice the difference between what's up to you and what isn't.
4. If it helps, just repeat a word in your mind each time you exhale and notice the way you're doing this voluntarily, and how other thoughts and feelings cross your mind involuntarily.
5. Observe your automatic thoughts and feelings from an

indifferent and detached perspective, without buying into them, as if you were studying the thoughts of another person.

Have a Maxim in Hand

Ancient Stoic students were told to have maxims or mottos always ready on hand to remind themselves to stay calm in the heat of the moment. As teachers, we can do this too. As alluded to in the above exercise, think of a word or phrase that you can use within a stressful situation to help remain calm. You can even put some of these maxims up in your classroom to remind yourself to pause and/or partake in cognitive distancing. Here are some short maxims that I use:

* Save it for later
* Now is not the time
* Some things are up to us and some things are not
* Rein in my judgement

Here is a more detailed maxim related to teaching that you can tell yourself as the students take their seats in the morning:

> *Today, I will be met with students who have no idea what I am going through. Knowing this, I will accept their shortcomings.*

Use the space below to come up with your own maxim(s):

Do Not Take Things Personally

If you have worked as a public school teacher, chances are you have been insulted by a student at some point. The Stoics advised us to remove our egos from the situation whenever we are faced with insults. What they meant by this is to not attach ourselves to the idea that the insults were personally directed at us. In my job, I get hurled a number of names at me every day. I do not take these names personally, however, because I know that some of my students have difficult home lives. In a weird way, I am relieved that they feel safe enough at school to verbalize their frustrations towards me, even if it is in an aggressive way. When I am met with an insult from a student, I reflect back to the following quote by Epictetus:

"Whenever someone does you a wrong or speaks ill of you, remember that he is doing what he thinks is proper. He can't possibly be guided by what appears right to you, but only by what appears right to him. So, if he sees things wrongly, he is the one who is hurt, because he is the one who has been deceived... Starting from this reasoning, you will be mild toward whoever insults you. Say each time, 'So it seemed to him' " (*Enchiridion* 42)

This quote is great because it reminds us to be patient with our insulters and realize that due to their current circumstance, they may have reacted in that way because they do not know any better. When we find ourselves met with insults, we should respond internally with patience and understanding, knowing that chances are the insult is a result of some other issue that is bothering the student. We have just been caught in the line of fire at this particular moment.

Adding Humour to the Situation

Epictetus said that "if someone tells you that so-and-so speaks ill of you, do not defend yourself against what he says, but answer,

'He did not know my other faults, or he would not have mentioned these alone' " (*Enchiridion*, 33.9). Seneca similarly wrote that "things should be made light of, and taken more easily: it is more civilized to laugh at life than to bewail it" (*On Tranquility of Mind* 15.2). I love these two quotes because they speak to the importance of not taking insults from others too seriously. I am sure that you have been in at least one situation where a student has insulted you directly or made comments about your pedagogy. The Stoics believed that we could at times respond to insults with self-deprecating humour. I tend to resort to this method a lot as a way to lighten the mood of the situation. I have been in circumstances, especially at my current job, where a student will try to get under my skin by making fun of my appearance. Recently, one student said I looked like Pennywise the clown at the end of the school day. I immediately turned to my educational assistant and asked, "I have not lost that much hair due to these kids yet, have I?" Adding humour to the situation helped me to detach from my initial feelings of anger and eventually respond to the comment in a more rational manner. If we decide to fight insults with insults, however, we not only increase the likelihood that the issue will get worse, but we also move away from living virtuously.

Conclusion

The Stoics provide us with great tools to deal with calming ourselves during stressful situations. Learning to detach from our immediate negative thoughts can go a long way towards helping us build mental fortitude. At the same time, know that implementing these strategies does not mean we are off the hook from disciplining or intervening when a student is being disruptive. Stoicism is not a quietist philosophy and should not excuse us from ensuring our classroom is a safe place for our students to thrive and grow. What we can do, however, is try our best to ensure we are in a healthy frame of mind to deal with the day-to-day obstacles that are thrown our way and not take thing so personally and seriously. Just remember that, to quote Epictetus, we are "insulted not by the person who strikes or abuses [us] but by [our] opinion that these things are insulting" (*Enchiridion* 20).

End-of-Chapter Reflection Questions

* When a student misbehaves in your school, what sort of emotions do you feel?
* Do these emotions tend to negatively impact how you handle the situation?
* Have you ever practiced mindfulness? Do you struggle trying to remain in the present moment?
* Think of the last student who insulted you. What reasons might have led this person to doing what they did?
* What motto can you repeat to yourself to help make light of a situation in class?

CHAPTER THREE

REFRAMING A "BAD DAY"

"If you are pained by any external thing, it is not this thing that disturbs you, but your own judgement about it. And it is in your power to wipe out this judgement now."

-Marcus Aurelius

During my first year of teaching, I remember leaving school many days feeling deflated. As mentioned earlier, I was faced with managing a lot of student behaviours. I would spend hours planning interactive lessons at night only to be met with comments such as how "school sucks" and so do I. I considered quitting my job on a number of occasions, believing that nothing good could come from this experience. Fortunately, I stuck with the job and, looking back, am extremely grateful for doing so.

We have all been there. Everyone has difficult days at work, and these difficult days can add up and lead us to question whether our job is the right fit. While I am not suggesting that we should stay in a job that does not provide us with a sense of fulfillment, I believe that we must take time to consider the role that our mind plays in interpreting the events that take place throughout our workday.

In *The Practicing Stoic: A Philosophical User's Manual,* William Farnsworth discusses this very issue. He explains that when we become distressed about something, there is a hidden chain of causalities that leads us to feeling the negative emotions that we do. Farnsworth suggests that after experiencing an event, we tend to create a value judgement about it, and then eventually adopt this judgement as reality rather than looking at the event from more of an objective point of view. Let's look at a classroom example to help illustrate Farnsworth's point here.

Say that you get a call one afternoon to supply teach for the second half of the day at a local elementary school. Upon arriving at the classroom, you notice that the students are running around, yelling back and forth, and ignoring you as you approach the absent teacher's desk to look at the lesson plans. As the day progresses, you have a difficult time settling the class down. There is a small group of students talking amongst themselves and half a dozen others who are on their cellphones. You attempt to quiet them down to focus but you notice that the more you try, the less responsive they become. By the time the dismissal bell sounds, your voice is almost completely gone. The students also dashed out and left a mess which requires you to spend the next twenty minutes tidying up the room.

Re-Evaluating Our Value Judgements

There are a number of ways that we can interpret the above situation. One is to adopt the value judgements that automatically pop into our heads. Another is to detach ourselves from these judgements. Since we are human, we cannot simply avoid having value judgements about things. For instance, if someone cut me off in traffic, I would instinctively presume the other driver is a careless person who does not deserve to be on the road. What I should do at a later time, however, is try to pick out the facts of the situation. So, this person cut me off. I doubt he did so in order to hurt me. Perhaps he is a beginning driver or just received bad news that caused him to be less vigilant in this particular instance. After all, I am sure we have been in the same position at some point. Marcus Aurelius reminds us of this idea when he writes that "whenever [we] take offense at someone else's fault, turn immediately to find the fault most similar in [our]self" (*Meditations*, 10.30). Reminding ourselves to be empathetic, even if we do not know the other person's situation, can go a long way in helping to develop a sense of inner calm.

After-School Reflection

In my own practice, I take the end of each school day to reflect on my impressions by journaling. I start by listing the facts of the day. For obvious reasons, some days I have a lot more to write down than others, especially if one of my lessons did not go according to plan or if I was met with a disruptive student who derailed the class. To complete this exercise, I create a three-column chart like the one below:

After listing the facts of the day in the left-hand column, I carefully examine the words that I used to describe things. If I used strong words such as "horrible" "annoying" or "awful". I cross them out or erase them from the "Facts of the Day". I do so not because these words are irrelevant to my reflection but rather because they are better suited to be written in the middle column titled "My Initial Value Judgements". The goal of the first column is to de-catastrophize these events, which means to write as objectively as possible when describing events.

In the middle column, I record my initial judgement(s) to each of the events that I listed under the "Facts of the Day". Since I am doing this in a journal that only I read, I do not hold back. I often am able to witness some of my hidden assumptions about certain students during this stage of the reflection. For example, I may write something like "Johnny is selfish since he never says 'Hi' back to me in the morning." To be as accurate as possible, I usually keep a small book with me during the day and write some of my initial impressions down when I have time (such as on breaks). I try my best to not filter what I write here but to remain as authentic as possible. After all, if I censor my thoughts, I am only short-changing the reflection process. If you decide to do this, make sure that you do not leave your book around for students to read!

Facts of the Day	My Initial Value Judgement(s)	Possible Reframes

How to Reframe

The third column requires us to reframe each event in a more positive light. To do this, I look for any silver linings or hidden possibilities that may have been made available to me because of my current circumstances. I also consider how my own value judgement could be mistaken. Here is an example of an activity I did while giving a presentation for a teachers college cohort a couple of years ago. Using the first row as an exemplar, take time to think/write about how you would initially respond to each fact and then trying reframing!

Facts of the Day	My Initial Value Judgement(s)	Possible Reframes
Brittany did not complete her homework.	Brittany is a lazy student.	Maybe Brittany was busy helping her mom at home last night.
Another teacher did not say "Hi" back to me in the staff room.		
After sitting in on one of my classes for an evaluation, my principal gave me a low score.		

I chose these above examples because they are common for many teachers, especially new ones in the field of education. There are many ways to reframe value judgements. One way is to think of the immediate positives that can come from the event. My first example in the above table does just that. If I do not get a job offer, I can be gracious that I was even given an opportunity to interview while also looking at this experience as beneficial because it allowed me to practice my interviewing skills. One can also think about future positives, too. For example, I may think that not getting this job will negatively impact my future, but I do not know that for sure. As cliché as it sounds, when one door closes, another door opens. I can eventually be offered an opportunity in education or even outside of the field that would have never been afforded to me if I got the job that I initially wanted.

Reflect on Our Responses

Besides writing just about events that happen to us during the school day, we can also reflect on memorable verbalized reactions (if we can remember them) that we had with students and other staff. Robert Marzano writes that when teachers experience new situations in the classroom triggered by a person, event, or task, we fall back on particular scripts that we subconsciously create for ourselves. For example, if we are teaching a math lesson and notice that a group of students are talking at the back of the class, we tend to automatically resort to a particular set of words that we often times verbalize out loud. In this example, it might be something like "Hey folks, make sure you are paying attention" or "This is the second time I have had to speak to you. Stop it!" The issue with subconscious scripts is that we risk "elicit[ing] a script on [our] part that is harmful or at least not very productive" (*Managing the Inner World of Teaching*, 38). This problem happens when we do not take the time to reflect on what sorts of scripts to use that can benefit the well-being of the student and class. Therefore, a good topic to think about at the end of the day is what sort of scripts we should fall back on if we encounter a particular event in or outside of the classroom.

Take the View from Above

In his *Meditations*, Marcus Aurelius says that we should "take a bird's-eye view of the world, as seen from above: its numerous gatherings and ceremonies, many voyages in calm and storm, and the different ways things come into being, take part in it, and cease to be" (9.30). He goes on to write that we must "reflect also on the life lived long ago by other people, and the life that shall be lived in foreign lands, and how many have never even heard your name, and how many will very soon forget it, and how many who now perhaps praise, will very soon blame you, and that neither memory nor fame nor anything else whatsoever is worth anything." Marcus here is describing a technique that the philosopher Pierre Hadot would coin many years later as the "view from above." The view from above involves removing yourself from a particular situation by pretending you are floating in the sky. For this mental exercise, you could zoom out as far as you would like. For example, you could look at your situation from the vantage point of the universe or even a different time period. The lesson to take away is that events and things are temporary and, compared to the scale of your entire life (let alone the entirety of the universe), will be forgotten. Using the "view from above" allows us to gain perspective on our issues and understand that they will pass at some point or at least become less pressing.

How can using this technique help with reframing a seemingly bad day at work? First off, you will realize that in the grand scheme of your career, this day will not mean anything and will be forgotten. For example, I am just a few years into my own career and I do not remember many events that took place during my first year of teaching. Besides this, you might realize that so many other people experience similar situations in the classroom around the world. This is why it is so important to find a mentor (I will discuss this in further detail in the next chapter) who can make this clear to you through the telling of their own history. So far in my young career, I have kept the mentality that the tougher the days, the better that this will benefit me in the long run. During my student teaching blocks, I worked with the most academic classes at the school. While I was certainty pushed to create intellectually driven lessons, I was not put into circumstances where I had to deal with much in the way of student behaviour.

In my actual teaching career, however, I have taught some difficult classes. While at first, I looked at this as a negative, I have come around to see these opportunities as moments that will, in the words of ultrarunner, author, and motivational speaker David Goggins, callus my mind. According to Goggins, callusing one's mind involves doing things that on the outside appear to be uncomfortable. This could come in the form of having that difficult conversation with a student to finally put his phone away because it is becoming a distraction in class or confronting a staff member who is making fun of another one behind her back. While we tend to associate callusing with something we want to avoid, there are many long-term benefits to it. One of these benefits is that without callusing our mind early in our teaching career, we will not be equipped with the mental and pedagogical tools we need to work in a variety of situations later on.

Give Yourself Advice

Another way to help reframe an event is to give yourself advice as if you were talking to your best friend or a child. The reason for this approach is because we tend to irrationally expect perfection from ourselves and overblow our mistakes, but we become more rational and compassionate when we are giving advice to our best friends or children.

To help illustrate this practice, write a letter to yourself about either a problem you encountered **today,** or a worry you have about the next day. If today went well and you are not worried about tomorrow, choose a past issue to work with. Pretend the problem belongs to someone else. Write advice on the next page using second-person pronouns and **your** name to give yourself advice. Take a look at the exemplar below for some guidance:

Dear Ryan,

I know you feel overwhelmed at work right now. You're juggling a lot of projects at once and there are a bunch of things competing for your attention.

It's no wonder you feel stressed. But it's not like this is anything new. You felt this way in the past, and it is unpleasant. But you are still at your job, and things are going well overall. This week may be unpleasant, but you get through it every time, and do your job well—or at least well enough!

So, get some sleep now. It will do you good!

Dear, _____,

_____

_____

_____

_____

_____

_____

_____

_____

_____

_____

_____

_____

Acceptance

While it is possible to reframe most events in life, there are going to be things that still continue to upset us (obviously, the death of a loved one is an extreme example of this, but it could also be that you walk into the staffroom and you unexpectedly hear a colleague spreading rumours about you). The Stoics would say that when we find ourselves in these situations, we should not suppress our feelings but accept the fact that we are experiencing them. "Acceptance means letting go of the rope," Robertson writes, "and stopping the futile struggle, so that you can get on with doing what's really important to you in life.Struggling with painful experiences often simply *escalates* them into more serious psychological suffering" (*Build Your Resilience,* 35). He says that "the best way to control them may sometimes be to stop trying, abandon the struggle for control, accept them, and allow them to come and go naturally over time" (ibid. 33). There is no doubt that you will not stay upset at a situation forever. If you do, counselling would probably be the next step to help alleviate some of the pain that you are going through. Most of the time, however, you will get over it.

A recent example of me practicing acceptance was allowing myself to feel the sadness that came with missing out on a job opportunity in my district. I was really hoping to get this job. In fact, I thought at the time that I was the only person qualified for it. As you could probably infer, I did not practice premeditating on adversity and was extremely disappointed when I found out that I did not get the position.Even after reframing, I still felt down, and so I gave myself permission to be upset by scheduling some time (around thirty minutes) in my day to feel the sadness. After this time was up, I told myself that I had to stop worrying about it until the next day's thirty-minute session. Sure enough, when September rolled around, this issue ceased to bug me anymore and I feel glad that things did not work out because I would not have gained the valuable experience at my current job.

Conclusion

Reframing and focusing on the things within our control are two of the most important Stoic practices. I recommend taking time to combine both practices while reflecting on your short- and long-term goals. You can use a chart like the one below to do so (I provided an example to get things started):

1. Goal you have for this year: ____Sign up to coach the school football team.____

2. How could it go wrong? ____Since I don't have much football experience, I can call the wrong plays during a game.____

3. If it goes wrong, what would be under your complete control?

____To remain calm during these situations and seek coaching advice from more experienced teacher.____

4. How could this be a good thing? ____I will inevitably improve as a coach by the season's end and possible build lasting relationships with my players.____

1. Goal you have for this year: _____

_____

2. How could it go wrong? _____

_____

3. If it goes wrong, what would be under your complete control?

_____

_____

4. How could this be a good thing? _____

_____

_____

End-of-Chapter Reflection Questions

* Do you find that your value judgements often negatively impact your mood and mindset?
* Think about a common stress that you deal with on a regular basis at school. Can reframing help with this stress?
* How can you uniquely practice the view from above?
* How do you go about providing your friends and/or family members with advice? What authentic words of encouragement or reframing approaches do you use?
* Do you struggle with acceptance? If so, why do you think this is the case? Do you think scheduling in time to experience these emotions will help you to accept your new circumstances?

CHAPTER FOUR

FINDING A ROLE MODEL

"Choose a [role model] whose life, conversations, and soul-expressing face have satisfied you; picture him always to yourself as your protector or your pattern. For we must indeed have someone according to whom we may regulate our characters; you can never straighten that which is crooked unless you use a ruler."

— Seneca

I am sometimes asked by prospective teachers what I believe to be the most valuable part of teachers college. Most people are a bit surprised with the answer that I give. In Canada, anyone who wants to be a qualified public school teacher must graduate from a two-year postsecondary program that involves successfully completing course work and a number of classroom placements. One might infer, therefore, that the teaching component of the program is most beneficial. After all, when else will you have the opportunity to teach in front of a group of students over a period of time? Sure, there are always volunteer opportunities within classrooms but due to many districts' strict certification standards, prospective teachers cannot simply deliver a lesson unless it is within the confines of one of these placements. My belief, however, is that the mentor teacher is the most valuable part.

Looking back, all of my mentor teachers were great in their own unique ways. I had one who was an expert on curriculum guidelines. He would spend time informing me of the new developments within Ministry documents and provide me with a number of useful resources that I continue to implement in my classroom to this day. I had another teacher who had one of the best rapports with his students that I have ever witnessed. During my time observing him teach, I was in awe of how he had his students listening on the edge of their seats to his every word. I could tell that they were actually having fun while learning and that they had tremendous respect for him.

Now, not one of my mentor teachers was *perfect* (whatever that is supposed to mean), but that is okay! I am grateful for how each taught me valuable lessons about the profession and even life. Something I am disappointed about, though, is how upon graduation, the emphasis on finding a mentor teacher disappears. There seems to be a belief that after we graduate teachers college, we can figure things out by ourselves. Many people presume that earning a freshly printed education degree means that we automatically have a number of innovative strategies we can draw from in our back pocket. Therefore, we should have no issues connecting with our students, creating fun and engaging lesson plans, and getting through the school day without dealing with different frustrations, right?

The Importance of Finding a Mentor

Although not all teachers agree with me about the value of mentorship, many do. I know this because many, especially those who are new to the field of education, have spoken to me about how they wish they could ask a more seasoned teacher to be their mentor or at least feel comfortable enough asking them about a variety of topics related to education. At the same time, some of these teachers that I have spoken to believe it is a sign of weakness to ask for help because it makes them appear that they do not have all of the answers. This line of thinking is ironic considering we teach our students to adopt a growth mindset, yet we do not do the same. Many also fear that they are bugging others if they ask for mentorship and that these seasoned teachers are too busy with their own responsibilities.

Mentors can be useful in a number of ways. Of course, there are teaching-related benefits. Mentors can share lessons plans or behavioural management strategies that have worked for them over the years. They can also share advice about employment-related matters. I still keep in contact with former teachers of mine (some of whom have become mentors) to get their unique perspectives on whether I should remain within a particular job or if moving to a different school or position would help me in the long run. It is always so valuable to listen to what they would say if they were in my shoes, as well as be able to hear their own unique and (many times) non-linear employment journey. Besides these topics, I love getting seasoned teachers' opinions about how to handle different mental stresses related to the profession. At the school where I am at now, I oftentimes touch base with another teacher about tips to stay calm if I find myself in a difficult situation with a particular student. It is reassuring to know that I can share my vulnerability about being fearful to teach a potentially high-risk student with another person instead of pretending that things are fine.

What Makes a Good Mentor?

Before getting into how to go about asking someone to be your mentor, let's address the type of person that you should be looking for while searching one out. Robert Greene, author of *Mastery,* and mentor to the Stoic writer Ryan Holiday, argues that "the best mentors are often those who have wide knowledge and experience" (106). He goes on to say that mentors can "perhaps provide what your parents didn't give you—support, confidence, direction, space to discover things on your own" (112). At the same time, and as mentioned in this chapter already, mentors are not perfect. In fact, the best are the ones who "have suffered to get to where they are" and experienced "doubts about their progress...[and] setbacks along the way" (116). These individuals provide the best mentorship because they understand, to allude to *New York Times* best-selling author Spencer Johnson's book title, that life is made up of peaks and valleys. Mentors can help to reaffirm that feeling upset after a certain incident in class is perfectly normal and, in many instances, needed to grow in the profession.

You may also realize that just one mentor may not be enough or that a particular mentor relationship will only be short lived. Greene says that "although one mentor at a time is best, it is not always possible to find the perfect one. In such case, an alternate strategy is to find several mentors in your immediate environment, each one fulfilling strategic gaps in your knowledge and experience" (107). On a personal note, one of my mentors is a good friend of mine who is a professional YouTuber. I consider him a mentor because he is very skilled in tech, such as video editing and audio clipping. In the past, I have asked to help or at least oversee what he does on the technical side of his job and this experience has helped me tremendously in the classroom. I now use many of the tips and tricks that I learned from him for creating tech-centred lesson plans. He did not, however, teach me anything about how to handle student behaviours in the classroom. Just because he cannot help me grow in all aspects of my job does not mean he is not a valuable mentor.

Take some time to think about who you would ask to be a mentor. Use the chart below to brainstorm and reflect on what beneficial characteristics they each have.

Mentor Names	Characteristics That Would Be Advantageous

How to Ask Someone to Be Your Mentor

Once you have narrowed down the person/people with whom you would like to ask to be your mentor(s), here are a few ways to approach them with the question:

1. **Play the long game**: Allow your relationship with your mentor(s) to grow organically. Maybe you want to mentor under the program chair of your department. You might be, however, new to the school and asking them to be your mentor right off the bat could feel uncomfortable. Take time to get involved in different school initiatives that the teacher is involved with. It will be beneficial for you because it will not only allow you to gain valuable knowledge and skills, but it will also allow you to strengthen your relationship with this person. Down the road, you can ask the person to be your official mentor.

2. **While asking someone, don't use the word *mentor***: I would say this approach is the most common one when asking another person to be your mentor. As mentioned previously, using the word "mentor" can be intimidating for some. At the same time, the mentor may feel that they do not have the time to take on this role. Mentors, however, do not need to be available all of the time. The relationship can be one that is predominately text- or phone-call-centred. Mentors and mentees also do not need to communicate every day either. Instead of directly asking someone to be your mentor, perhaps you say something to the degree of "I notice you are really good at _____. This is an area of my teaching where I am lacking. Is there a chance that we can meet around your schedule so that you can show me how to be better at _____?" This approach is a little less intimidating, no?

3. **Flat out ask the person to be your mentor**: This is the most direct approach. As a result, you may get the most direct answer. I wish that our school culture promoted this type of questioning more but, as mentioned earlier, there is a fear about admitting that we need to work with a more experienced and seasoned professional to help grow in our field. I was a part of the New Teacher Induction Program (NTIP) a couple of years ago in my district and the thing that I loved the most about it was it required all beginning teachers to seek out a mentor and schedule meetings and observational periods to encourage professional development. I remember that when I first approached my mentor, he was honoured. I know that most teachers would feel the same way if they were asked because it would be a sign of respect that they are doing something right in their field. I learned so much from this mentorship and, though we do not talk as much today, I feel comfortable

enough to give him a call at any point to ask for his feedback on a particular school-related issue.

What to Do if You Cannot Find a Mentor

There is a chance that because of certain reasons outside of your control, you may not be able to find a mentor. In these circumstances, there is a Stoic technique that you can use to help simulate or create one. To help us strive towards our highest self, we can contemplate a sage. A sage is an ideal or real-life role model (except one that we do not communicate with) who we can refer to for guidance throughout our day. For example, the Stoic philosophers used Zeus as their sage and would continually contemplate his positive characteristics to help navigate them through difficult situations. They would ask themselves questions like "What would the sage do?" similar to how many Christians ask, "What would Jesus do?" You can also piece together your unique, Frankenstein-like, sage who is made up of people that you look up to in your life. Maybe you respect the patience that your mother exhibits on a daily basis and the initiative that your younger brother displays. All that matters is that you have some sort of sage in mind, whether it be a close friend, relative, fictional character, historical figure, or any combination of them.

People I Admire	Characteristics I Admire in Them

Take some time to come up with your own sage. Use the chart on the previous page to help you.

After you have chosen a sage, imagine that the person is sitting on your shoulder, watching what you do and giving you some honest feedback. Think back to a time when you did not behave as you may have liked at school.

Write out what aspect of your character you would like to improve upon. Think about how your sage would have acted in the same situation. This is a great exercise taken from the previously mentioned *A Handbook for New Stoics*.

EVENT	HOW DID I BEHAVE?	HOW WOULD MY SAGE HAVE RESPONDED?

Next, reflect on what steps you have to put in place to strive towards cultivating some of the positive characteristics that your sage has. One thing to keep in mind is that your sage is meant to be somewhat unrealistic, meaning you will not necessarily be able to fully embody them. Instead, contemplating the sage motivates you to always strive and learn how to better yourself.

STEPS TO CULTIVATE YOUR SAGE'S POSITIVE QUALITIES

_____

_____

_____

_____

_____

_____

_____

Choose Your Company Well

Besides modeling ourselves after noble figures, another way that we can work towards reaching our highest selves is to choose our company well. In the *Enchiridion,* Epictetus says that we should "refuse the entertainments of strangers and the vulgar. But if occasion arise to accept them, then strain every nerve to avoid lapsing into the state of the vulgar" (33.6). In this passage, Epictetus is warning us to be careful with the types of people that we come to associate with in life. If these people have a pessimistic outlook of the world, there is a chance that we will start adopting these mindsets without even noticing it. During my short career, I have been in situations where staff at certain schools were not enthused to be there. They may look for every little problem and do not think about the benefits of teaching. When I encounter these people, I try my best to think that they may just be frustrated due to a difficult issue they are facing and still believe that their profession has meaning. There comes a point, however, when you may want to distance yourself if you find that they make a continual habit of complaining. While you may want to slip in little comments here and there to remind them about the rewarding aspects of the job, it is not necessarily your place to convince others about the benefits of teaching. Instead, slowly separating yourself from the negativeiy may be your best bet.

Conclusion

This chapter all comes back to fostering a growth mindset. We must realize that teaching, like any other worthwhile endeavour, takes a lifetime to master. Therefore, we must be willing to admit when we do not have all of the answers and seek out others for guidance. Marcus Aurelius knew the importance of this idea. Book 1 of his *Meditations* outlined all of the lessons learned from different people who made an impact on his life. At the same time, we must also remember that we serve as role models to our students and should be willing to share with them how we reflect and regulate our own behaviour to help us reach our best selves.

End-of-Chapter Reflection Questions

* What areas do you need to work on to better yourself as a teacher?
* Who are your role models in education?
* Do you consider any of these role models to be mentors as well?
* When during the day can you find time to contemplate your Stoic Sage?
* Do you think the staff that you associated with at school are positive or negative influences on you?

CHAPTER FIVE

DEALING WITH IMPOSTER SYNDROME

"How much trouble he avoids by not looking
to see what his neighbour does or thinks—
by looking only to what he does himself,
that it may be just and pure."

— Marcus Aurelius

O ne of the most common things to be worried about as a teacher
is thinking that you are not good enough to be working at
your job. One of my professors from graduate school, Barbara K.
Seeber, writes about this very issue in her book *The Slow Professor:*
Challenging the Culture of Speed in the Academy. Imposter syndrome—or as Seeber calls it, "academic shame"—is "the intensely
painful feeling or experience of believing that we aren't as smart
or capable as our colleagues, that our... teaching isn't as good as
that of our colleagues, that our comments in a meeting or at a
speaker event aren't as rigorous as that of our colleagues, and
therefore we are unworthy of belonging to the community of great
minds" (87). While Seeber is talking about professors working in
academia, public school teachers can feel similar feelings of shame
as academics do, just in slightly different ways. For example, a

fellow colleague may share her lesson plans with the rest of the staff and after looking at them, you feel that her work is better than yours. This idea is later intensified when you hear other staff members praising her lessons. On another occasion, you may attend a staff meeting and propose a few ideas for an upcoming school fundraiser and no one backs you. As a result, you might believe that you have nothing to offer and should just keep quiet for future meetings.

Stop Worrying About Other's Opinions

Marcus Aurelius wrote that many times "we have more respect for the opinions our neighbours hold about us than we do for our own" (*Meditations,* 12.4). This idea becomes even more problematic when we do not actually know the opinions of others but instead just assume what they might be. As we looked at earlier, worrying about externals can bring about unnecessary stress and anxiety. If we are inferring what another co-worker thinks of us, there is a decent chance that our inference(s) will be inaccurate. I used to infer others' opinions of me all of the time, especially that of my administration. If someone is not as friendly as they usually are in the hallway or a student refuses to do work, do not just assume it is due to resentment. There are a number of different reasons that could explain these particular behaviours.

In the activity on the next page, try recording times when you worried about another's opinion of yourself while at school. Consider the different reasons for why the person behaved this way. I have included my above example below to help illustrate the exercise:

The Problem with Comparing Ourselves to Others

We have all compared ourselves to others at some point or another. We seem to always be in competition with others about a number of things. While people tend to believe that teaching is a profession that is exempt from unhealthy competition, this has certainty not been the case in my experience. We can look no further to the job market.

Trying to find a teaching job in the public sector, at least in my region of Canada, is very different from other occupations. Many

Event	My Initial Inference	What the Actual Reason Might Have Been
A fellow staff member was not friendly with me while we passed each other in the hallway.	This person does not like me, perhaps because I am new.	She could be in a rush or is having a bad day at home and therefore does not want to be overly friendly.

of my friends in other fields got hired by companies and organizations right after graduating and while they may have started with a lower, entry-level salary, they had consistent work at one central location and prospects of moving up to higher paid and more fulfilling positions. The process for teachers is different. If a candidate is hired by a school board, they must work as a supply teacher for a full-year, which requires them to fill in for absent teachers at different schools everyday (that is, if they even get a call for the day), before being able to apply to contract-type jobs. These contract jobs, which are typically called long-terms, are temporary positions that are created in order to cover a teacher who is off sick, on maternity leave, etc. Long-terms can range anywhere from a few weeks to an entire year depending on the absent teacher's situation.

While a full-year long-term sounds like a pretty good gig, it has its downfalls. For example, the absent teacher can return unexpectedly at any time, thus kicking the replacement out; this happened to me during my first long-term experience. As well, long-terms do not get paid on holidays, spring break, or in the summer as permanent teachers do. Long-terms are also usually pressured to take on several duties outside of regular school hours, whether it be coaching numerous sports teams or sitting as a staff representative for the student and parent councils. In the past, I have coached basketball, hockey, helped with band practice, and supervised several lunchtime and after-school clubs. I am not saying that I regret getting involved in any of these extra-curricular activities (in fact, I view each of them as rewarding experiences that I had fun doing), but trying to balance so many commitments at one time can be both physically and mentally draining, especially considering that we are still required to uphold our classroom obligations of lesson planning and marking student work. Many beginning teachers believe they need to stretch themselves in a million directions and continually take additional qualification courses to remain competitive in the market. The issue becomes that this line of thinking can not only lead to burn out but force teachers to feel like they have to undercut each other to take jobs away or block each other from getting jobs. While I first thought that this problem exists mostly in the corporate world, the longer I have been in education, the more I see it becoming more present here.

The Stoics emphasize that everyone is on their own path and therefore comparing ourselves with others will only lead to unnecessary stress. In my current teaching position, I used to compare how my students engaged with my lessons against how other teachers were engaging their students. If another class was productive one day and mine was not, I would assume it was because I was not as good of a teacher and therefore I would never become a permanent hire. When I let go of this mindset and acknowledged that every class is made up of different students and therefore it is unreasonable to compare ourselves with others, I was better able to perform at my job and actually enjoy it more. Not too long after, I also got on full-time.

Seek Our Own Praise

In his letters, Seneca writes that we should "be [our] own spectator; seek [our] own applause" (*Letters from a Stoic*, 78.21). Epictetus similarly said that "when someone is properly grounded in life, they shouldn't have to look outside themselves for approval" (*Discourses* 1.21). Seneca and Epictetus are emphasizing here that we should not be indebted to someone else for praise but instead rely on it ourselves. Though it is always nice to get complimented by our administration, we know firsthand whether we are putting in a good effort in our jobs or whether we are cutting corners and not doing our best. Outside praise should not signal to you that you are doing a good or bad job. Instead, find moments to lift yourself up. I try to do this as often as I can with positive self-talk. At times when I am going through a difficult period, I even schedule time out of my day to do so.

Complete the below exercise by thinking about when you can give yourself some praise and what you can say to yourself (this could be something like a maxim):

When I Could Practice Self-Praise	What I Could Tell Myself

Conclusion

Dealing with imposter syndrome is not fun. As Stoic teachers, we need to continually remind ourselves that the only person we should be in competition with is ourselves. We should strive to be better every day and respect that our colleagues are on their own separate paths. As I mentioned earlier, adopting a growth mindset can help to manage feelings of inferiority because we will consider ourselves a work in progress and therefore always on the road to improvement.

End-of-Chapter Reflection Questions

* Do you tend to compare yourself with other teachers? If so, what makes you do this?
* Have you ever dealt with imposter syndrome? What caused you to feel you were not good enough?
* What are some examples of unhealthy competition in your job?
* Do you seek praise from others?
* Do you ever praise yourself?

CHAPTER SIX

PRACTICING STOIC SELF-CARE

"People try to get away from it all — to the country, to the beach, to the mountains. You always wish that you could too. Which is idiotic: You can get away from it anytime you like. By going within. Nowhere you can go is more peaceful — more free of interruptions — than your own soul."

— Marcus Aurelius

In *The Teacher Self-Care Manual: Simple Strategies for Stressed Teachers,* Patrice Palmer highlights a number of research studies that found teachers to have one of the highest burnout and turnover rates of any profession. I have been hearing about these types of studies since I was in university, though I mostly ignored their relevance to my future at the time. It was not until I officially entered the profession that I began to understand why teachers so often leave education within their first five years. As teachers, we always have to be *on,* meaning if we are facing difficulties in our personal life, we must try our best to prevent these issues from influencing how we behave in front of the class. As well, our job can be super unpredictable. Many teachers can learn last minute that they have to teach a course that they have never taught before. At my job, I can get new students enrolled in my classes at any point throughout the semester due to them being suspended or expelled from their high school.

Because of all these things, it is important to carve out time for self-care. Palmer references the below definition by Jason Newell and Gordon MacNeil in her book to help define what she means by self-care. According to Newell and MacNeil, practicing self-care involves using the appropriate "skills and strategies...to maintain personal, familial, emotional, and spiritual needs while attending to the needs and demands of others" (3). Palmer emphasize how "self-care is not an indulgence" but is "an essential component of prevention of exhaustion and/or profession burnout" (4). In fact, she suggests that teachers who regularly practice self-care tend to be more emotionally resilient.

Self-care obviously looks different for everyone. It can mean going for a walk, watching your favourite show, or getting together with friends. I cannot tell you what to do for self-care, but the advice I can give, as highlighted in Stoic philosophy, is to try your best to take a minimalist approach to your schedule so that there is time for it. While the Stoics did not necessarily address self-care as we have come to know it today, they did stress the importance of making good use of the time we have on earth. We may have possessions, but all of these things can be replaced. Time is the only thing that we can never get back.

This reality, however, does not mean that we have to fill up every waking minute of the day with being productive. Instead, we need to know how to manage our schedule to be able to flourish in the areas of our life that are most important to us. Doing so will help us cultivate a more meaningful life, something that is very different from having a busy life. We need to become more conscious of what we spend our time doing and not doing (for example, are we neglecting spending time with family and friends because we are always trying to get ahead on things like marking or answering student emails?). In his essay "On the Shortness of Life", Seneca echoes this idea when he writes how "everyone hustles his life on and suffers from a yearning for the future and a weariness of the present" (11). He finds it peculiar how we are greedy in the sense that we so often refuse to give our money to those in need yet on the other hand we freely give away our time to obligations that do not add much fulfillment to our life.

Similar to what you might do when going through a crowded closet, figure out what obligations can be tossed away in order to help minimize stress and maximize fulfillment. This process is especially important to apply to your teaching commitments. Maybe you coach four different teams, are on two committees, and are planning on taking on an additional qualification course on the side (I have been in this situation many times before!). Instead of saying yes to everything and continuing on the path to burnout, take the time to reflect on what you can cut out. Use the below prompts to help you through it:

Committment: _____

Does it provide joy or meaning?   YES   NO

If no, what plan can you put in place to remove/adjust it within your schedule? _____

_____

Committment: _____

Does it provide joy or meaning?   YES   NO

If no, what plan can you put in place to remove/adjust it within your schedule? _____

_____

Committment: _____

Does it provide joy or meaning?   YES   NO

If no, what plan can you put in place to remove/adjust it within your schedule? _____

Memento Mori

To help motivate us to be more aware of the limited time that we have on earth, the Stoics advised that we should reflect on the fact that we will die one day. Seneca wrote that we should "rehearse this thought every day, that [we] may be able to depart from life contentedly" (Letters to Lucilius, 4.4-5). Contemplating death helps to internalize the idea that it is a natural and inevitable process. It does not mean, however, having a morbid fascination with death. Instead, this exercise reminds us that our time is limited. We will stop taking things for granted and will be more aware of what we want to spend our time on.

Take the time to reflect on your mortality. Imagine you had one year left to live, and complete the following example: create a bucket list of the top five things you still want to do in your teaching career. After doing so, think about whether the schedule that you currently following can allow you to do these things or whether changes may have to be made.

1.

2.

3.

4.

5.

How does this exercise relate to teacher self-care? We should always keep a critical eye on whether our various commitments are helping us move towards or away from our best self. When examining the above list, does anything surprise you? Are you setting up your life in a way that can allow you to check these things off our bucket list? Knowing that we are mortal and only have a short time on time can help us realize that we need to focus on the most important things in life and learn to drop the non-essentials.

Adding Stillness to Our Days

One of the most powerful books I have read in the past few years is Ryan Holiday's *Stillness is Key*. Not only is this book filled with fantastic wisdom from the Stoics and different Eastern philosophers, but it contains a variety of stories focused on many notable people throughout history who learned to take time to step outside from the business of life. Holiday's argument is that all of these people had one main thing in common that helped them attain their goals and live a virtuous life: a willingness to cultivate mental stillness. He outlines the following steps we should take:

* Be fully present.
* Empty our minds of preconceptions.
* Sit quietly and reflect.

Surely, taking time to put aside the hectic pressures of our job and simply *be* can go a long way to fostering a calm and tranquil mind, which can help to alleviate stress. Are you deliberately carving out time in your day to do so? If you are not, coming up with cues can help to signal to yourself when it is time to abandon life's worries and just be with yourself can be useful. Use the below chart to help identify what cues can help you practice stillness (I have added my own example to get the ball rolling):

CUE	HOW I WILL GO ABOUT PRACTICING STILLNESS
When I approach the photocopier at the end of the school day.	Rather than photocopying for tomorrow's lessons right away, I will look out of the window and admire the neighbouring houses. I will try to stop thinking for two minutes and practice mindfulness.

The Inner Citadel

The Stoic believed that you can practice stillness anywhere. Seneca asked, "How can the sight of new countries give you pleasure?... Do you want to know why your running away doesn't help? You take yourself along. Your mental burden must be put down before any place will satisfy you" (*Epistles* 28.2). Just like

Marcus's opening quote at the beginning of the chapter, Seneca is reminding us that changing up our external environment does not always release us from stress. Instead, we have to focus on internal transformation. The Stoics had a concept they referred to called the *"Inner Citadel"* to help highlight this idea. The writer Pierre Hadot describes it as creating a fortress within us where nothing from the outside can agitate or disturb us. Hadot notes that the Inner Citadel is not there from the beginning of our lives but is built and constantly reinforced over time.

Think of the Inner Citadel as your favourite place to visit where none of your problems can reach you. The main thing is that this place is within rather than being somewhere external. As teachers, it is good to cultivate an Inner Citadel where none of your emotional baggage from the school day is allowed to enter. You can start by carving out five minutes each day to tell yourself that you are retreating to your Inner Citadel. It is probably best to do so when you are alone and will not be distracted by others. I do this when I enter my car at the end of the school day; after all, no one can call me down to the office over the PA system and students cannot search me out to ask questions about their work. I find that as long as I put my phone away, I can sit in my car for five minutes to get away from all of the stresses of the day. Try to develop your own Inner Citadel. Know that it can take years and a lot of practice to find at least one moment during the day where you will not be perturbed by intruding thoughts. However, it is never too late to get started!

Conclusion

In *The Art of Living: The Classical Manual of Virtue, Happiness, and Effectiveness*, Sharon Lebell writes that "philosophy's purpose is to illuminate the ways our soul has been infected by unsound beliefs, untrained tumultuous desires, and dubious life choices and preferences that are unworthy of us. Self-scrutiny applied with kindness is the main antidote" (n.p.). We should take this approach when it comes to self-care. We have to be willing to make the changes necessary to live our best self but at the same time be okay with forgiving ourselves when we fall short. Falling short provides us with many life lessons, one of them being that we might be taking on too much at this time or overidentifying with some external event. As teachers, we work our best when we are well-rested and focused on the task at hand. In order to do so, we need to only care about the things that are most important to us and let go of the non-essentials.

End-of-Chapter Reflection Question

* Do you carve out intentional time for self-care every week?
* How is self-care promoted at your school?
* What does self-care look like for you?
* What is one thing in your schedule that you can get rid of in order to free up more time for yourself?
* Do you find it difficult to practice mindfulness? If so, what are other ways you can go about practicing presence (i.e. playing an instrument, reading, writing, etc.)?

CHAPTER SEVEN

RESOURCES FOR PROFESSIONAL DEVELOPMENT

"That's why the philosophers warn us not to be satisfied with mere learning, but to add practice and then training. For as time passes we forget what we learned and end up doing the opposite, and hold opinions the opposite of what we should."

— Epictetus

As I mentioned in the preface, Stoicism is a popular topic of discussion today, especially amongst young people. There are various books, as well as online resources, that cover the philosophy in many unique ways. I thought I would take this chapter to provide you with some Stoic professional development resources in case you want to explore more about the philosophy than what was mentioned in this book. After all, learning more about the philosophy itself will help you to better practice being a Stoic teacher.

Books About Stoicism

There are a number of excellent authors who have written about Stoicism for a more public audience. The first book I ever read about Stoicism was by William B. Irvine titled *A Guide to the Good Life: The Ancient Art of Stoic Joy*. Irvine is great at not only providing an overview of the first Stoic philosophers (including the big three that I have been alluding to throughout this book) but also gets into the many cognitive exercises that the Stoics are known for practicing. Donald Robertson's book *Stoicism and the Art of Happiness: Practical Wisdom for Everyday Life* is similar in its approach except it gets more into the historical background of the philosophy.

If you are more into narrative storytelling rather than an expository text on the philosophy, Robertson's *How to Think Like a Roman Emperor* is a great book to explore because it gets into the biography of Marcus Aurelius, including some dramatized scenes from Aurelius's life (the last chapter on death is very beautiful to read!). Staying on the genre of narrative storytelling, Massimo Pigliucci's *How to Be a Stoic: Using Ancient Philosophy to Live a Modern Life* is also fantastic because it includes a series of imaginary conversations between the narrator and Epictetus to help illustrate how the Ancient Stoics would tackle topics like friendship, love, and loneliness, amongst others. If you like learning about how Stoicism has helped to influence different figures from history, I would recommend anything from Ryan Holiday (especially *The Obstacle is the Way* and *Ego is the Enemy)*. He also recently wrote a great book called *Lives of the Stoics* where he focuses specifically on the early Stoic thinkers, especially those who are outside of the big three. Holiday also has a big social media following and has a great podcast called *The Daily Stoic,* where he interviews various thinkers, athletes, and celebrities about how Stoicism has helped to shape their worldview.

If you are interested in reading any of the original Stoic texts, I would recommend the *Meditations* first. I find that it is the most readable out of them all and is also the most fascinating and intriguing given that we are reading Marcus's own personal journal. He does repeat himself a lot (something that has been criticized by some). I actually do not mind the repetition, however, because it helps to ingrain the key principles of the philosophy in my head. After reading the *Meditations,* you may want to check out Epictetus's *Discourses* since the text contains short snippets out his lectures and you can read them in a nonlinear way based on a particular topic that you are interested in learning about. When it comes to Seneca, many people would recommend his *Letters* before any of his other writings. For myself, I sought out his essays (such as *On Anger* and *On the Shortness of Life*) and believe them to be a better place to start.

The Stoic Community

Due to the growing popularity of Stoicism today, we are lucky to have many groups and initiatives out there to help connect people from all walks of life to the philosophy. Stoicism is a philosophy meant to be lived out, not just studied. Based on this belief, there exists a not-for profit organization called the Stoic Fellowship that helps practicing Stoics from all over the world meet up to talk about the philosophy and its relevance in the 21st-century. The group was founded by Gregory Lopez and if you visit www. stoicfellowship.com, you can check to see if there is a local group near you!

There also exist many social media pages that focus on Stoicism and allow members to interact with each other as well as with prominent Stoic writers and thinkers. The largest one can be found at www.facebook.com/groups/Stoicism. As of 2021, it has over 85 thousand members. The Facebook group is great because members can ask questions they have about Stoic philosophy or its relevance to a particular topic and other members tend to comment. There are also other ways that different types of social media have promoted Stoicism. Two podcasts that I listen to regularly are The Walled Garden Podcast (formally The Practical Stoic Podcast) and The Sunday Stoic (I have had the privilege to guest host on the latter one). Both have had phenomenal guests come on over the years to share how Stoicism has changed their life. As well, there are times where the regular hosts provide listeners with short yet rich meditations inspired by the works of the original Stoic thinkers. Gregory Sadler also has a great YouTube channel to check out if you are interested in some of the more obscure topics related to Stoicism (such as Stoic physics and lesser-known thinkers related to the philosophy). Simply type in Gregory B. Sadler on YouTube to check out his awesome channel!

There are also great Stoic events around. One such event is Stoicon. Every year, a Stoicism-based conference is held at some place in the world (even with the pandemic, the event still went on, except virtually of course!). It is a great way to listen to some of the leading Stoic thinkers of the day as well as have an opportunity to ask them questions that you have about their work. Writers that I've talked about in this book attend so it is well worth the trip! If you Google "Stoicon," you will get all of the information that you need. Stoic Week is also an amazing event that takes place annually which is free to the public. It is run online and since 2012 has had over 20 thousand people participate in it. If you register, you will be sent a handbook to help meditate on a particular Stoic principle per day as well as practice using a specific exercise. Studies have been conducted about Stoic Week and have shown that people are happier and more satisfied with life by the end of the week. If you are interested, visit www.modernstoicism.com. While you are there, be sure to check out all of the great blogs and articles about a variety of topics related to the philosophy, from parenting to politics. You can also check out an article that

I co-wrote with a good friend of mine called "Stoic Students: How We Are Learning to Let Go of Worry and Find Peace."

Conclusion

This chapter was by far the shortest yet possibly will serve as one of the most useful for some. The bottom line is that in order to be a Stoic teacher, we must be willing to do our homework and learn more about the philosophy, thinkers, and important principles that we can apply to our daily lives. There are a whole host of resources out there to help us strive towards our highest potential. I recommend asking around your school to see if anyone would be interested in starting a Stoic group. What I have found is that when you have other people to keep you accountable, it is easier to follow those four Stoic virtues outlined in my introduction. At the same time, know that it is not enough to just read and talk about these principles and virtues. As Marcus mentions, we have all the tools within, and it is our job to live a life where they are made manifest. "Dig deep; the water—goodness—is down there," Marcus writes, "and as long as [we] keep digging, [they] will keep bubbling up" (*Meditations*, 7.59).

End-of-Chapter Reflection Questions

* How do you learn best (i.e.. books, YouTube videos, podcasts, etc.)?
* What aspect(s) of Stoicism do you want to learn more about?
* What Stoic community in the chapter interests you the most?
* How can you start a Stoic community in your area?
* How can you introduce the principles of Stoicism to your colleagues and/or students?

CHAPTER EIGHT

A SPOTLIGHT ON STOIC TEACHERS

"Don't explain your philosophy; embody it."

— Epictetus

During the early stages of writing this book, I envisioned having a chapter where I included first-person narratives written by educators in order to illustrate how Stoicism helps them remain resilient in their jobs. At the time, I was unsure whether I would be able to network with such people, let alone have any of them agree to write something about this topic Thankfully, I was able to find a number of educators who wished to contribute. The individuals featured in this chapter do a marvellous job at illustrating how Stoic philosophy has many benefits for teachers from all walks of life. They also have something important in common; they are not just familiar with Stoic principles but also try their best to live them out! Enjoy!

ADVICE FROM A MIDDLE SCHOOL TEACHER

The utility of Stoicism in the classroom is a topic that is almost guaranteed not to appear in any course syllabus in college educational courses. While there are many topics we learn about ranging from differentiation to behavioral management, our pedagogical higher education includes very little (if any) about teacher mental health and well-being. That being said, the great thing about using Stoicism in the classroom is that it is a fantastic way to settle disputes between students, as well as create a mindset for the teacher as an individual who has an important role to play to the next generation.

As many educators know, the classroom is full of disputes between students. Some of us can honestly (and sometimes humorously) admit that there is not a week that goes by without a student getting into a disagreement about another person stealing his or her pencil. The Stoics saw one fundamental thing that is necessary for a healthy view about things and events: the ability to come to objective and reasonable judgments about things. One of the great ways to do this in student disputes is by separating the students involved and to go through Socratic questioning. Socrates, of course, was (in)famous about asking leading questions to get to a more objective point of view. His questions also had the benefit of leading the interlocutor to more accurate conclusions. This is a great technique for settling disputes. For example, you may ask the pencil thief, "Why did you feel the need to take his/her pencil?" and "Do you think that taking his/her pencil is the best way to act?" For the victim of this situation, you might ask them, "Should we be upset about everything that happens to us?" and "When someone steals from us, what is the most useful thing for you to do?"

Apart from the usefulness of Stoicism while dealing with students, there are many ways I've used Stoicism in order to make sense of the importance of my current role. There were days that were admittedly more difficult than others and in those times, I would always use the Stoic technique of the "view from above."

This practice allowed me to see the critical role that I played in society. I imagined, for example, the interconnected implication of being an educator. How many people, I thought, will ultimately be influenced by what I teach my students today? Even though this number is impossible to quantify for sure, the effect is massive. Also, on the other hand, what would the world look like without educators? Our societies would simply collapse, and our cultures would denigrate into something akin to what the boys experienced in *Lord of the Flies*.

Bob Cymber is a former middle school teacher and owner of Stoic Coach. He resides in St. Louis, Missouri, and has been practicing Stoicism for nine years. During his philosophy undergrad, he was required to read Marcus Aurelius's Meditations. From that initial exposure, he trained to apply Stoic principles to deal with his clinical panic disorder, ADHD, depression, and OCD. He now facilitates mental training programs that apply these principles. His website is www.stoiccoach.net.

THE STOIC VIEW FROM ABOVE

Teaching can be very difficult. Many of us work long hours designing lessons, marking, and doing professional development.. Add reports, parent teacher interviews, supervisions, etc., and it becomes apparent that teaching is not simply a career, but rather, a lifestyle. Every generation of children puts forward their own sets of challenges. Likewise, best practice changes, as do curriculum, society, and technology. All that considered, I think it is fair to say that sometimes this profession can be overwhelming.

However, just as Stoicism can guide us in our day-to-day lives, it can also aid us in our teaching practice. What follows are three Stoic tools that all teachers should consider in their approach to education.

One important Stoic tool all teachers could benefit from involves taking a few minutes out of the day to sit back, reflect, and meditate while considering the larger picture or the view from above. By doing this we can start to appreciate the role we play and the impact we have in the lives of our students. Without us, there would be no future doctors, lawyers, or teachers; we shape society and inspire young people to not only follow their dreams, but also, to identify what their dreams are. By taking time to view the world from above, we can see that the work we put in with its various challenges is of vital importance to society.

A second Stoic tool we need to embrace is the Stoic notion of control and how many of the challenging factors we face fall outside of our purview of what we control. We need then to focus on what is in our control, which is our attitudes towards our students, our subjects, and the important function we play. We need to understand that although many of the systemic factors we experience as teachers that impede us may be outside of our control, that this is no excuse to slack on the things that are under our control. Rather, we must only focus on what we can change and influence. We need to focus on asking ourselves important questions like: are the systemic barriers that are impeding me or my students within my ability to change? If they are not, then we are wasting precious time and energy fretting about them. This is not to say that we should not advocate and engage in activities that will raise awareness and possibly change these obstacles, but we should always focus the bulk of our daily efforts on working best within the system we have, not the one we wish existed.

Lastly, a final practice which all Stoic teachers should keep in mind is gratitude for what we have and how far we have come. Rather than feel frustration, anger, or hopelessness at the obstacles that impede our everyday ideal practice, we should take some time to consider all we have despite these impediments. Imagine what it would be like teaching under worse conditions than you currently find yourself in. Imagine working longer hours with less resources and more pressure and see how actually, although your current situation may not be ideal, it is far from the worst you could find yourself in.

In summary, three practices that I believe are essential to finding tranquility and success in the teaching trade are Stoic meditation, understanding Stoic notions of control, and lastly, gratitude for what we have. These tools have kept me humble and provided me with the resilience I need to approach each day in an honest and open way ready to serve the needs of my students and advocate for their success, and I hope that you find them just as useful in your practice.

Michael Burton is a secondary long-term occasional teacher with the Peel District School Board in Ontario, Canada. His work has been featured on Modern Stoicism and he occasionally writes on his blog https://stoicteacher.wordpress.com. He can also be found on Twitter as @stoicteacher.

FIVE TIPS FOR THE STOIC MINDFUL TEACHER

There is much that I have learnt from Stoicism, a journey that I embarked on with the gift of a Roman bust in Dubai in 1998 and my reading of Donald Robertson's book, _How to Think like_ *a Roman Emperor*, in April of 2019. For now, I'll focus on five ways in which I teach and practice Stoic wisdom and resilience:

1. **Seneca, "Each day is a life": Intention Setting and Gratitude**

Seeking to live each day with *prosoche*, what Epictetus in his discourse "On Attention" advises as a daily continual practice of mindfulness, I begin with the acknowledgment of the continued gift of a precious human life. I acknowledge the brevity and impermanence of my human existence, the intention to live it well, and to be of benefit to all sentient beings. I remind myself of the cardinal virtues of Stoicism: wisdom, justice (kindness), courage, and temperance (moderation).

2. **The Delphi Maxim, "Know Yourself": Stoic Journaling and More**

In *The Artist's Way*, Julia Cameron writes that in our morning pages "the snowflake pattern of our soul emerges." Journaling is a way of knowing oneself and living an "examined life." In my Stoicism, mindfulness and creative writing classes, I encourage students to keep a journal.

3. **Dispassion and Engagement**

The principle of dispassion and engagement is one that I was familiar with prior to my introduction to Stoicism. Mahatma Gandhi, drawing on the wisdom of the Bhagwat Gita, spoke of 100% effort and 0% outcome. But as I immersed myself in Marcus's *Meditations*, this truth become an ongoing practice in my work as a teacher and writer: "You will give yourself relief...if you perform every action as though it were your last, freed from... dissatisfaction with what is allotted to you. You will see how few are things that a person needs to master if he is to live a tranquil and god-fearing life;" (2:5).

4. **The judgement of others is an "external"**

In grade five, I knew that I wanted to be an English teacher like my mother, Sarah George. I have taught at universities in the U.S., Oman, UAE, and Canada. I received the Excellence in Teaching Award (2019, School of Continuing Studies, University of Toronto) and most student feedback is praise. On occasion there is a comment that feels harsh, even hurtful or ignorant. I have learned to exhibit patience and examine if there is a kernel of truth in the negative critique, wisdom that I can garner to improve my teaching. If none, I say, as a good Stoic would, "it is nothing to me," and continue in my efforts to be well-prepared, knowledgeable, present and compassionate with my students.

5. **Daily Review**

Drawing from *The Golden Verses of Pythagoras*, at the end of each day, I ask myself these three questions: How did I do? What did I omit to do? What could I have done better?

I model myself on Seneca: "When the lamp is taken out of my sight, and my wife, who knows my habit, has ceased to talk, I pass the whole day in review before myself, and repeat all that I have said and done. I conceal nothing from myself, and omit nothing" (*On Anger*).

Some say that this Stoic focus on self-improvement takes us away from life itself. I, on the other hand, see mindful living as a fulfilling, wise, and happy life: *eudaimonia*.

Ranjini George holds a PhD in English Literature from Northern Illinois University, USA, an MA in English Literature from St. Stephen's College, New Delhi, and an MFA in Creative Writing from the University of British Columbia, Canada. More recently, she won the first place in Canada's inaugural Coffee Shop Author Contest for her travel memoir, a work in progress, Miracle of Flowers: In the Footsteps of an Emperor, a Goddess, a Story and a Tiffin-Stall.

She was an Associate Professor of English at Zayed University, Dubai, in the United Arab Emirates where she founded and ran the Teaching with the Mind of Mindfulness series. She currently teaches classes; classes such as Stoicism and the Good Life; Dear Diary: Marcus Aurelius, Anne Frank and Thich Nhat Hanh; Mindfulness, Stoicism and Writing for Discipline and Productivity; and, Meditation and Writing at SCS, University of Toronto. In 2019, she received the SCS, University of Toronto Excellence in Teaching award. Her book Through My Mother's Window: Emirati Women Tell their Stories and Recipes *was published in Dubai in December 2016. Website:* https://ranjinigeorge.wordpress.com

KEEP CALM AND TEACH ON

The Stoic philosophers teach us to concentrate on our internal world while taking proper action in the external world. According to Epictetus, everyone has multiple roles in life. My roles include that of father, husband, son, and teacher. I must reflect on these roles in order to know how to take proper action. Teaching is hard work. Despite the challenges, I consider myself fortunate to be a biology teacher. This vocation offers many unique ways to practice Stoic philosophy on a daily basis. Fair treatment and assessment of students is a form of justice. I apply wisdom when I alter my teaching styles to reach the class, and when I teach students about the living world and our connections to it. It also takes a certain amount of fortitude and temperance to grade lab reports in a timely fashion and survive the onslaught of students who question their final grades at the end of a semester.

Many of the student-learning outcomes that I strive for are

ultimately out of my control, so I can really only focus on what I can do, and then do it to the best of my ability. I remind myself that I must work to make the content clear, explain it enthusiastically, and assess their knowledge in a fair and non-judgmental way. I cannot make a student care about the material, but I can provide an example of someone who does. I cannot make a student study, but I can be a mentor when they try and do not achieve the grade they desire. My job is not to be the emperor of the classroom, someone to be feared, but to work with the students, "like the upper and lower rows of teeth" to make learning possible.

Steve Karafit is a husband, father, podcaster, and a lecturer in the Department of Biology at the University of Central Arkansas.

STOICISM MAKES ME HAPPIER IN THE CLASSROOM

I was fortunate, through upbringing and training, to develop a Stoic mindset even before I was aware of the philosophy. I believe Stoicism has preserved my happiness and effectiveness as a teacher through trying times.

Virtue is the most challenging aspect of my Stoic practice in the classroom. Time, after all, is my most treasured teaching resource, and putting "first things first" often means sacrificing time on the altar of "the right thing." We all lost teaching time during the 2020/21 school year, and my 8th grade math students suffer for it. So, I decided to sacrifice a chunk of time (and curriculum) in order to reteach basic concepts while simultaneously extending the smallest group. It's the "right thing," but it's difficult. I have to stay present and only seek to control what I have power over.

On good days, I remain in the moment. Decisions are easy and distractions are discarded.

There are tough days, however. Let's face it, a classroom full of preteens presents a cauldron of challenges: behavior, distractions, attendance issues, social issues, etc. And often the challenges arise from my own life. I have a small business that collapsed during 2020, am going through a divorce, and have three adolescent daughters of my own. *Memento mori*, or "remember that you will die," is my rallying cry on these days. It reminds me of the saying, "This, too, shall pass." All situations, all things, good and bad, are temporary. So, I have developed over time the habit of enjoying every moment as much as I can. This habit often allows me to smile through ridiculous student behavior or poorly timed absences or rude emails.

I live in a chaotic environment. Some of it is my doing, most of it is not. Either way, the resulting noise could bury me in self-obsession and self-doubt if not for the daily touchstones of humility and radical presence provided by my Stoic practice. Instead, I laugh with my students, am present with others, and look for simple moments of happiness in my life.

Jeff Macloud is a teacher and entrepreneur in Northern California. He has taught many subjects and all grades from K - 12 in some capacity, but is currently teaching middle school language arts and math. He created Napa STEM Academy in 2018, a company that provided STEM enrichment in school and after school for K-5 students. A victim of COVID distancing precautions, Napa STEM Academy is currently restructuring. Prior to teaching and entrepreneurship, Jeff served nearly 25 years in the United States Air Force, flying various aircraft and serving as a flight instructor and leader. Jeff has two master's degrees and a bachelor's degree.

He was born and raised near New Orleans, Louisiana, and now lives with this three daughters in Napa, California.

GRATEFUL FOR THIS (TEACHING/LEARNING) MOMENT: JOURNEYING FROM PERFECTIONISM TO STOICISM

As a teacher, I model what I teach, blurring the line between my personal and professional worlds. In my young years, I searched for perfection and optimism in life, work, and relationships. I wished I could teach my students everything I knew about science, such a fascinating and poetic teaching subject. I wished I could tell the world, my family, and my friends how amazing and fortunate they were for being alive. I wished I could laugh without crying, run without resting, and succeed without failing.

Over time, reading philosophical works and living through war and immigration, I transformed my being in the world from perfectionism to Stoicism, which I encountered not only in the works of Epictetus, Seneca, Marcus Aurelius, and Anthony de Mello, but also in different religious teachings such as Christianity and Buddhism. As I was awakening in a world where my control is limited, my death inevitable, my failure educational, my appreciation of life healing, and a true friend scarce, I was becoming more content with my life as a mother, friend, refugee, newcomer to Canada, and teacher.

Three decades ago, I was teaching elementary school science in a war-torn Yugoslavia. Once a week, I would leave my school and travel with several other teachers to a small village in the immediate war zone to teach a split class of Grade 7 and Grade 8 students. A few of my colleagues complained about this dangerous task. I didn't. I was a teacher, and my job was to teach. I was aware that my control over life events is limited and my destiny uncertain (whether in a time of war or in a time of peace) and I decided to give it my best—to teach, comfort, and inspire my students by doing what we can control (learning and teaching), by remembering who we are (teachers, learners, and humans) and what we value (knowledge, life, and relationships), and by reflecting on and appreciating our learning process without sweating over exams and grades that will not necessary make us good and content people. Being present in a teaching/learning moment resulted in knowing beyond academic knowing, in appreciating life, in prioritizing today over yesterday and tomorrow.

I feel blessed for being given the opportunity to wake up as a human being and a Stoic teacher during the difficult times of war, refugeehood, and re-settlement. Being present in a moment and being grateful for that moment remained my teaching philosophy.

Dr. Snežana Obradović-Ratković is a research officer and instructor in the Faculty of Education, Brock University, Ontario, Canada. She is a science teacher from the former Yugoslavia who immigrated to Canada in 1998, after the Yugoslav Wars. Her scholarship focuses on migration and indigeneity, transnational and transdisciplinary teacher education, decolonizing and arts-based research methodologies, academic writing and publishing, and well-being in higher education.

WHEN STOICISM MEETS ZEN

Years before the publication of my book *The Zen Teacher: Creating Focus, Simplicity, and Tranquility in the Classroom*, I was going through a particularly rough patch of life and a teacher friend complimented me on the admirable quality of my "stoic" approach.

I'd heard the word before, but I wasn't completely sure what it meant. So the first thing I did, of course, was head to the dictionary. And thinking back, it's quite possible it was an actual dictionary. But looking online now, I see that there are two basic definitions for Stoic: 1) *adj.* a person who can endure pain or hardship without showing their feelings or complaining and 2) *n.* a member of the ancient philosophical of Stoicism.

I suppose my friend was right. I didn't see a lot of reason to trouble people with what I was going through and even though the general situation was challenging, I was always aware that many (most?) of the individual moments of my life were pretty great, even transcendent on occasion, and despite the current turbulence, I was grateful for them.

Now, after having studied such topics as Zen and mindfulness—and yes, even Stoicism—I do see that there is some general overlap: embracing acceptance, taking responsibility, living in the moment, expressing gratitude, practicing focus, and cultivating a sense of peace. All excellent approaches that the people I like best (and those I most admire) try to put into practice.

Dan Tricarico been a high school English teacher for over twenty-five years. He is also the author of The Zen Teacher: Creating Focus, Simplicity, and Tranquility in the Classroom (DBC, Inc. 2015) and Sanctuaries: Self-Care Secrets for Stressed Out Teachers. In his spare time, he enjoys writing fiction, listening to music (especially roots, rock, and the blues), reading mystery novels, staring out of windows, and watching movies. One of his first loves is writing poetry, and he has published many poems both in print and on-line.

LESSONS FROM A ROMAN EMPEROR: MARCUS AURELIUS IN HIS *MEDITATIONS*

There are so many things I have learned from Marcus Aurelius, starting from the moment I discovered his *Meditations*. Over the years, I have owned many small paperback translations, always underlining the lines that touched my heart at that moment. These quotes still fill me with awe and wonder at the Roman emperor's deep humanity and wisdom.

Here I have compiled a few of my favorites, with short explanations of how they still resonate for me daily. I bring these and other Stoic quotes into the classroom often, and give the students time to react, think about, discuss and debate how these thoughts may touch their hearts.

> *"Everything we hear is an opinion, not a fact.*
> *Everything we see is a perspective, not the truth."*

This quote reminds me that my job is teaching young people to question and interrogate what they hear. I want the next generation to see the world through other people's eyes, and to imagine that their own viewpoint is one amongst many, and not necessarily the "truth," but still valid as a perspective.

> *"What we do now echoes in eternity."*

The future of the world depends on these young people, and what I do makes a difference in the long term. Respecting the ties from today to the future is both powerful and gives me a sense of my responsibility to be first a good person, today and every day.

> *"You always own the option of having no opinion.*
> *There is never any need to get worked up or to*
> *trouble your soul about things you cannot control.*

These things are not asking to be judged by you.
Leave them alone."

Being a teacher and admitting that you do not know the correct answer or do not have an opinion sends a powerful message to a young person. It means that adults are not all-knowing and all-powerful. I like bringing this perspective into the classroom because it contradicts what students think adults should know. When I use this quote, I often like to discuss how powerful it is to separate yourself from what you think or feel, and to give up needing to be right. There is often strength in recognizing that you have weaknesses.

"For it is in your power to retire into yourself
whenever you choose."

Stoics believe that to a certain extent we can control our own thoughts, but we cannot control the thoughts or actions of others. I like to emphasize that we can turn off the negative chatter from the outside world and see our own minds as a shelter where we are safe. It is also important to realize that teachers and students must make time every day for recovery from the school environment, which can be brutal. For me, this quote is not about social isolation and loneliness, but really about self-care and mindfulness.

"Remember that very little is needed to make a
happy life."

When I read this quote, I always think about how it was written by one of the world's most powerful men at that time. Even Marcus was in pursuit of a happy life, and he realized that the power to live well was in his own control. Teaching may not bring much money, fame, or gratitude, but it can bring a happiness in knowing that the future generation has been given a small gift of inner strength.

Amy Valladares, PhD, discovered ancient Stoic philosophy as a freshman in college, and then rediscovered it during a midlife crisis. She credits her natural Stoicism to the school of hard knocks, getting her through some tough times. Amy's anthropology training has led her to self-study the ancient sources, take part in modern community-building, and create a personal Stoic practice. She co-organized the Stoicons in New York (2016), Toronto (2017), London (2018) and Athens (2019). She coauthored the 2021 Stoic Week for Students on ModernStoicism.com. As a teacher of middle- and high school students, she has stealthily incorporated ideas of Stoic philosophy into classes about everyday life.

End-of-Chapter Reflection Questions

* Which teacher's advice sounded closest to your own principles?
* Which teacher's advice appealed to you as something you might change in the future?
* How will it inform your teaching or your attitude in the future?
* Was there any passage that surprised you?
* Can you think of a colleague of yours who would benefit from Stoicism?

TEACHING AS A PROCESS

"When one is busy and absorbed in one's work, the very absorption affords great delight; but when one has withdrawn one's hand from the completed masterpiece, the pleasure is not so keen. Now it is the fruit of his art that he enjoys; it was the art itself that he enjoyed while he was painting"

— Seneca

When I was in high school, I was interested in studying classical piano at the postsecondary level. I loved the idea of one day being a classically trained pianist and getting the chance to play at different performance halls around the world. There was only one problem with this goal. In order to enter any postsecondary music program, I needed to have a successful audition, write a theory test, and also have good grades. While I met the last two criteria, I certainly did not have the first one. I finally gave up on my goal, not necessarily because I could not do it—after all, I had been playing piano since I was six and heard of many people with a nonclassical background grind it out for a year or two in order to do well on the qualifying audition. Instead, I knew I was more interested in the *idea* of going to school for classical piano than actually wanting to put the effort into practicing.

What this experience has taught me is that any worthy endeavor requires perseverance, hard work, and an openness to fail. The same thing is true for wanting to be a good teacher. We cannot be a good teacher without a willingness to embrace the growing pains of the job over the span of many years. You may feel that you are dynamic coming out of teachers college, but you simply have not been in those unique situations that test not only your intellect but also your patience. Becoming a talented teacher involves a lifetime and then some. If you talk to the greats, you will notice that they never say that they have mastered the profession. Instead, they will refer to the journey and how they may feel that some days they take one step forward but then the next they take two steps back. As Stoic teachers, we must embrace the ups and downs of this process and adapt the mentality that we will never be perfect at what we do.

The Analogy of the Stoic Archer

The Stoic philosopher Antipater used an analogy about archery to help explain the importance of focusing on the process rather than the end result. He said that we must think of goals in the way that an archer would view hitting the target. The archer cannot guarantee perfect aim (for example, there can be a high wind that day) but can perform the proper steps (such as using the correct technique, stance, etc.) to increase the percentage of success. This idea all comes back to the dichotomy of control. As teachers, this is, in my opinion, the most central Stoic principle to be practicing on a consistent basis. In his essay "Stoic Teaching and Stoic Control," Michael Burton says that "by acknowledging the idea that students' attitudes are not something in the scope of the teacher's control, teachers can begin to ask the right types of questions, and plan the right kinds of lessons, in order to bring about better learning outcomes for their students" (120). When I read this quote, I see the idea of the Stoic archer at work. As teachers, if we continually worry about the things outside of our control, we will not be in the right state of mind to do our best in the classroom. "Unfortunately, there are going to be some pupils," Burton writes, "who, despite your best efforts, will see no value in what you are trying to do." In my current teaching position, this sentiment holds true every day. Due to external factors (such as my students' home lives, past history, diagnosed or undiagnosed learning disability), I simply cannot make the difference that I hope to. Instead, I will always fall short. Being okay with this reality will go a long way to being a wise, Stoic teacher.

Embrace Failure and Uncertainty

Seneca writes that "the condition of life is that of a bathhouse, a crowd, a journey: some things are thrown at you, others just happen by accident. Life is not a dainty affair. You have started on a long road; inevitably you will stumble, you will knock into things, you will fall..." (*Epistles* 107.2) This quote highlights how we must be prepared to meet the obstacles of life. Our careers are uncertain. Cuts can be made, we can switch classroom and/ or school against our will, and many other unpredictable events can crop up. To truly be a Stoic teacher means to strive every day towards our best selves, to cultivate equanimity as often as possible when faced with challenges, and be willing to—in the words of the Irish playwright Samuel Beckett— "fail again, fail better."

BIBLIOGRAPHY

Aurelius, Marcus. *The Meditations*. Translated by Gregory Hays, Modern Library, 2003.

Berg, Maggie and Barbara K. Seeber. *The Slow Professor*: *Challenging the Culture of Speed in the Academy*. University of Toronto Press, 2017.

Burton, Michael. "Stoic Teaching & Stoic Control." *Stoicism Today*: *Selected Writing* I, edited by Patrick Ussher, 2014, pp. 119-121

Epictetus. *Discourses and Selected Writings*. Translated by Robert Dobbin. Penguin, 2008.

Greene, Robert. *Mastery*. Penguin Books, 2012.

Farnsworth, Ward, *The Practicing Stoic*: *A Philosophical User's Manual*. David R. Godine, 2018.

Goggins, David. *Can't Hurt Me*: *Master Your Mind and Defy the Odds*. Lioncrest Publishing, 2018.

Irvine, William. *A Guide to the Good Life*: *The Ancient Art of Stoic Joy*. Oxford University Press, 2009.

Holiday, Ryan, and Stephen Hanselman. *The Daily Stoic*: 366 *Meditations on Wisdom, Perseverance, and the Art of Living*. Portfolio/Penguin, 2016.

Holiday, Ryan. *Lives of the Stoics: The Art of Living from Zeno to Marcus Aurelius*. Portfolio/Penguin, 2020.

---. *Ego is the Enemy*. Portfolio/Penguin, 2016.

---. *The Obstacle is the Way*. Portfolio/Penguin, 2014.

---. *Stillness is the Key*. Portfolio/Penguin, 2019.

Johnson, Spencer. *Peaks and Valleys: Making Good and Bad Times Work for You—At Work and in Life*. Atria Book, 2019.

Lebell, Sharon. *The Art of Living: The Classical Manual on Virtue, Happiness, and Effectiveness*. HarperOne, 2007.

Lopez, Gregory and Massimo Pigliucci. *A Handbook for New Stoic: How to Thrive in a World Out of Your Control*. The Experiment, 2019.

Lucas, Lisa J. *Practicing Presence: Simple Self-Care Strategies for Teachers*. Stenhouse Publishers, 2017.

Marzano, Jana and Robert Marzano. *Managing the Inner World of Teaching: Emotion, Interpretations, and Actions*. Solution Tree, 2015.

Quesada, Donna. *Buddha in the Classroom: Zen Wisdom to Inspire Teachers*. Skyhorse Pub., 2011.

Palmer, Patrice *The Teacher Self-Care Manual: Simple Self-Care Strategies for Stressed Teachers*. Alphabet Publishing, 2019.

Pigliucci, Massimo. *How to be a Stoic: Using Ancient Philosophy to Live a Modern Life.* Basic Books, 2017

Robertson, Donald. *Build Your Resilience: CBT: Mindfulness and Stress Management to Survive and Thrive in any Situation.* John Murray Learning, 2019.

Robertson, Donald. *How to Think Like a Roman Emperor: The Stoic Philosophy of Marcus Aurelius.* St. Martin's Press, 2019.

Robertson, Donald. *Stoicism and the Art of Happiness: Practical Wisdom for Everyday Life.* John Murray Learning, 2018.

---. "A Simplified Modern Approach to Stoicism." *Donald Robertson*, 3 Feb.2013, donaldrobertson. name/2013/02/ 03/a-simplified-modern-approach-to-stoicism/.

Seneca. *How to Keep Your Cool: An Ancient Guide to Anger Management.* Translated by James S. Romm, Princeton University Press, 2019.

---. *Letters from a Stoic.* Translated by Robin Campbell, Penguin Books, 2004.

---. *On the Shortness of Life.* Translated by CDN Consta, Penguin Books, 2004.

Tricarico, Dan. *The Zen Teacher: Creating Focus, Simplicity, and Tranquility in the Classroom.* Dave Burgess Consulting, Inc., 2015.

ABOUT THE AUTHOR

RYAN RACINE is a high school teacher and college instructor from Canada. He earned his master's of English language and literature from Brock University and has published in magazines such as *Modern Stoicism, PACE, The Ekphrastic Review,* and *University Affairs.*

www.ingramcontent.com/pod-product-compliance
Lightning Source LLC
Chambersburg PA
CBHW020919140626
46545CB00015B/893